$ 295

The Devins Award
Poetry Anthology

The Devins Award Poetry Anthology

Edited by Gerald Costanzo

with a Foreword by George Garrett

University of Missouri Press
Columbia and London

Copyright © 1998 by Gerald Costanzo
University of Missouri Press, Columbia, Missouri 65201
Printed and bound in the United States of America
All rights reserved

5 4 3 2 1   02 01 00 99 98

Library of Congress Cataloging-in-Publication Data
The Devins Award Poetry Anthology / edited by
    Gerald Costanzo.
        p.   cm.
    ISBN 0-8262-1161-5 (alk. paper)
    1, American poetry—20th century.   I. Costanzo. Gerald.
PS615. D47 1998   97-40959
811'.5408—dc21   CIP

♾™ This paper meets the requirements of the American
National Standard for Permanence of Paper for Printed
Library Materials, Z39.48, 1984.

Printer and binder: Thomson-Shore, Inc.
Typeface: Palatino

For William Peden

Contents

Publisher's Note

The University of Missouri Press, like the greater artistic community of America, has been indebted to the family of Dr. George Devins since 1965 when the Devins Award in Poetry was first awarded and funded by that family. For thirty years, celebrating the work of twenty-nine poets, the Devins family has committed itself to the art and craft of contemporary verse. That unending commitment has extended itself through the publication of this anthology, which has been generously subsidized by the Devins family.

The University of Missouri Press is proud to acknowledge the family's ongoing support, without which some of the poets this anthology might not have been published, and also to acknowledge the family's financial contribution to the publication of *The Devins Award Poetry Anthology*. Without such private support, poetry in America would not have thrived.

Beverly Jarrett
Director and
Editor-in-Chief

Foreword

You aren't going to believe this. I didn't at the time, when it was happening. Once upon a time, 1985 or thereabouts, I was asked to be the judge for the Devins Award and, as well, for the Breakthrough Series for short fiction. The press thought there might be a hundred or so manuscripts to deal with. Fine. Then one day a UPS truck showed up in my driveway. "Where do you want these?" the driver asked. "In the house or the garage? I'd recommend the garage." Plain truth is that there was a whole truckload of boxes from Missouri—several hundred large boxes, each filled with many manuscripts. Filled up my garage, they did. You can imagine what the so-called judging process, a month or so before the deadline, was like. Actually, I'm pretty proud, proud and pleased with my selections; the Devins winners I picked were *The Bus Home* by Shirley Anders Bowers and Nancy Schoenberger's *Girl on a White Porch*.

I mention this, though, to demonstrate the need for this award. It filled a major need. The absence of it is already, and will continue to be, a serious loss for American letters. This anthology, generously put together by Gerald Costanzo, is at once a testimony to the quality and importance of the Devins Award and a memorial to it. This is a wonderful list of first-rate poets. Behind them are the competition, the shadows of many good poets, several of whom may not yet have found a home for their work. This anthology salutes them, too.

George Garrett
Charlottesville, Virginia

The Devins Award
Poetry Anthology

Introduction

The first book of poems Missouri ever published contained stories as well: *Poems and Stories* by Thomas McAfee. Published in the fall of 1960 and issued in a paperback edition, it contained forty-three poems, some of which had previously appeared in *Prairie Schooner,* the *Beloit Poetry Journal,* the *New Mexico Quarterly,* and other magazines. The collection concluded with six stories, which had also gained publication—in *The Dial* and *Contact.* And one, "The Prisoner," had been published in the April 1959 issue of *Esquire.*

William Peden, professor, scholar, novelist, and author of short fiction, founded the University of Missouri Press in 1958. Peden's wife, Margaret, reports that early in its existence, when anyone would inquire as to the location of the press, Peden would joke that it was in the bottom drawer of the desk in his English department office. During 1958, Peden set about producing the first Missouri titles, which appeared at the beginning of 1959: *The White Hound,* stories by Ward Dorrance and Thomas Mabry, with an introduction by Caroline Gordon; *Seventeenth Century Songs and Lyrics* by John Cutts; Julian A. Steyermark's *Vegetational History of the Ozark Forest;* and *The Wild Mammals of Missouri* by Charles W. and Elizabeth R. Schwartz.

It was always Peden's intention that the Press support "creative" as well as scholarly and regional books. In the publisher's foreword to *Poems and Stories* he stated:

> This collection of poems and stories by Thomas McAfee is the first in a projected series of work by new young writers to be published by the University of Missouri Press. In America today the young writer is confronted with the peculiar and potentially destructive dilemma: more and

more . . . writers are creating meaningful
poetry and fiction at a time when rapidly spiral-
ling costs make it increasingly difficult for them
to reach a national audience. With its "New
Writers Series," the University of Missouri
Press hopes, in a modest way, to present to a
national audience representative selections from
the work of such young writers.

Peden had been, as far back as the forties, a cham-
pion of the short story, and he was one of the few indi-
viduals (along with critic Ray West) who continually
reviewed story collections and encouraged their publica-
tion. His seminal book on the subject, *The American Short
Story*, was widely read, and one of his own collections,
Night in Funland, was, in the late sixties, the first publica-
tion in Louisiana State's continuing program in short
fiction.

A book of George Garrett's stories, *Cold Ground Was
My Bed Last Night*, was the third original creative work
among the approximately forty titles that Missouri had
produced by the spring of 1964. The second book of
poems (following McAfee's) was Nancy Sullivan's *The
History of the World as Pictures*. This title, selected by three
judges—Reed Whittemore, who was serving at that time
as Consultant in Poetry to the Library of Congress;
Harold Whitehall; and Donald Justice—inaugurated The
Devins Award.

The award, publicized variously as The Devins
Memorial Award (1965-1970), The Devins Poetry Award
(1971), and The Devins Award for Poetry (1972-1994),
was formulated from conversations among members of
the Kansas City literary community as early as 1961. Dan
Jaffe, a young faculty member at the University of Mis-
souri–Kansas City and later founder of the prestigious
BkMk Press, initiated discussions with Thorp Menn, the
arts and entertainment editor of the *Kansas City Star*,
about creating a series that would bring noted contempo-

rary poets to the city to read their work. The Kansas City Jewish Community Center agreed to participate; beginning in 1962, the center hosted five evenings of readings each year in its American Poets Series. In 1963 the first of the Kansas City Poetry Contests was announced. Coordinated by the center's "Poetry Committee," the contests (offered in "High School," "College," and "General" categories) were administered with funds donated by the *Star,* by Hallmark Cards, Inc., and by manufacturer's representative H. Jay Sharp. Subsequently, Thorp Menn brought together two of his friends, Robert Morris, the director of the University of Missouri Press, and Dr. Edward Devins, president of the Jewish Community Center and patron of its reading series, for conversations that culminated in a book-publication award. In 1965 The Devins Award became "the major prize" of the Kansas City Poetry Contests and, following the Yale Series of Younger Poets (founded in 1919), the second "first book" poetry prize in America.

Missouri began publishing its Breakthrough Books, a successor to Peden's New Writers Series, in 1969 under the directorship of Thomas Lloyd. The series included each year's Devins collection, along with selected other poetry and short fiction titles, in each instance the author's first book in the particular genre. Missouri's publication of fiction, no longer limited to first books, continues to be influential and exemplary to the present day. The procedure for choosing the Devins winner changed in 1974, with the Press assuming full responsibility for the selection of judges. While the Devins Award was affiliated with the Kansas City Poetry Contests, panels consisting of two to five judges selected the winners via "anonymous" readings; that is, the names of the entrants did not appear anywhere on the manuscripts forwarded to the judges. Beginning in 1974, poets were issued invitations to submit their manuscripts based on the presentation to the press of a personal résumé and a complete publication record. The statement of purpose, which was printed at the beginning of each Devins selection, was amended slightly with the publication of my book late in that year; with the updating of the winning title and author, it remained substantially the same for the next twenty years:

> *In the Aviary* is the 1974 winner of The Devins Award for Poetry, an annual award originally made possible by the generosity of Dr. and Mrs. Edward A. Devins of Kansas City. Dr. Devins was former President of the Kansas City Jewish Community Center and a patron of the Center's American Poets Series. Upon the death of Dr. Edward Devins in 1974, his son, Dr. George Devins, acted to continue the Award. Nomination for the Award is made by the University of Missouri Press from those poetry manuscripts selected by the Press for publication in a given year. In 1974 the manuscript of Gerald Costanzo was among three selected for publication from more than 100 invited manuscript submissions, and was subsequently nominated by the Press for the Devins Award.

In the early eighties the Press settled on a system of appointing a single judge to make the selection of all the Breakthrough Books to be published during a two-year period. By 1995, when Missouri discontinued the publication of poetry, it had brought into print more than sixty poetry titles. The most famous of them—interestingly, not a Devins selection—is Annie Dillard's *Tickets for a Prayer Wheel*. A first-edition copy in fine condition sells on the rare book market for between $500 and $600, though I saw one recently in the Caliban Book Shop in Pittsburgh that was signed and bore an inscription to one of Ms. Dillard's prep school English teachers, priced at $900!

Certainly the Breakthrough Series brought to fruition William Peden's vision of fostering the work of young writers. Devins winners have found the award to be of inestimable value in launching their writing careers. The majority of them have continued to publish collections of poems; several have published collections of short fiction, as well as novels and books of nonfiction. Three poets whose first books were Devins winners or Breakthrough selections went on to establish or edit poetry series at other university presses. Indeed, I used the check Dr. George Devins presented me on the snowy Monday evening of December 2, 1974, to publish the first Carnegie Mellon University Press poetry titles in 1975.

The first Devins winner, Nancy Sullivan, told me, "The night I heard that I'd won the award a telephone call delightfully interrupted a party I was giving for Galway Kinnell after a reading he had given at the University of Rhode Island. I flew first class—for the first and last time in my life—to Kansas City to receive the award, which was presented by Dr. Devins and Langston Hughes. After the presentation, I went with Langston Hughes to hear some great Kansas City jazz." Diana O'Hehir remembers, "I was on my way to a reception to meet the new president of my college, an institution where I felt unproven, unpublished, and certainly untenured. I peered into my mailbox, deciphered the return address on the envelope, and thought, 'Oh my God, another of *those* (Rejections—I'd been getting a lot of them). And now I have to go in there and impress this new administrator.' Which, after I read the letter is what I *did* do, by dashing into the reception and greeting the lady with 'Guess what!' The new president was impressed enough to kiss me. The Devins Award was the first real recognition I'd had; it was my first book publication and, most of all, the first 'professional' validation of my ability. It gave me a tremendous boost emotionally and it sparked my writing; I still feel happy when I think of it."

Janet Shaw (who won when her name was Janet Beeler) says her invitation to read at the Kansas City Jewish Community Center on the night she was presented with the award read . . . *we have some exciting surprises to add a little something special to your reading!* "The surprises were two ballet dancers and a harpist to accompany my reading of the poems. I would read a poem through a first time, then, during my second reading, their harpist and dancers would improvise their interpretation. Some of the audience were recent immigrants who spoke little English and they, especially, beamed at the harpist strumming and the dancers leaping all around me—'Ah, so this is poetry in America!' The audience applauded heartily after each 'number,' and afterward I received many compliments on my pink mohair sweater. It was a blast!"

Awards bring additional good fortune, according to Jonathan Holden: "I was a graduate student getting a Ph.D. in American Literature at the University of Colorado when I won the prize. I had submitted my manuscript on a lark, after seeing the poster advertising the award in the CU English Department. At the time, I was building a geodesic dome in the foothills above Boulder; hence the book's title, *Design for a House*. . . . I was amazed to learn that I had won the prize, and winning it changed my life radically for the better. When I gave the Devins reading, Betty Littleton, a fiction writer and an instructor at Stephens College, in Columbia, Missouri, was present, and she immediately recruited me to my first job after I graduated in 1974."

Ed Ochester commented, "I had published a number of chapbooks, and had gotten some praise from writers such as Edward Field, whose work I loved, but winning the Devins meant that two excellent poets (Michael S. Harper and Mark Strand) who had never heard of me had selected my manuscript over zillions of others. . . . I know a lot of writers, and I've heard some bravado to the contrary, but I don't know anybody whose life wasn't strengthened and made sweeter by the selection of his or her first book by a major press. It isn't just the imprimatur, though that's a part of it; it's having the work available to readers and one's sense of vocation confirmed. That's why first-book contests such as the Devins have an importance much greater than their frequently meager sales."

Nancy Willard wrote me: "When I arrived at the airport in Kansas City, I climbed into a taxi and the driver asked me where I was from.

"'I flew here from Poughkeepsie.'

"'Poughkeepsie!' He shot me a dark look. 'Are you one of them outside agitators?'

"I thought: I'm a poet and aren't all poets outside agitators?

"But the political event he had in mind was the arrival of Hubert Humphrey, not my poetry reading for the Devins Award."

Wesley McNair had been sending his first book manuscript out for four years before he learned he had won the prize. "I'd begun to feel a little like Willy Loman with his sample case. Discouraged about my prospects, I hardly believed the news, responding, I was told later by my caller from the University of Missouri Press, in frozen monosyllables. But I was all thawed out by the time the press mailed the galleys of my new book to me a few weeks later, urging me to return them as soon as possible. . . . To manage, I had to take the galleys with me to the college where I worked then, a thankless place whose faculty were routinely overworked and underpaid. I carried my volume-to-be, composed during hours stolen from correcting papers, into committee meetings like an anarchist with a bomb. In the end, my Devins Award provided much more than a first book: it gave me proof that neither rejection nor the daily grind had got me; that against the odds, I had become a poet." G. E. Murray expressed similar feelings: "I got the good news by mail. I'd been previously informed that I was one of three finalists. When the letter finally arrived, my wife called me at work to see if she should open it. Why not? So when the news sunk in, I thought it only right to leave work, get a bottle of champagne, and celebrate with my wife. Which I did. The next day I learned what had happened during my unexpected absence from the office that afternoon: the firm had been taken over. Well, companies get bought and sold every day. But there was only one 1979 Devins Award winner!"

A highlight of my own experience involved the fact that I was, concurrent to submitting my manuscript to Missouri, serving as a preliminary reader of poetry manuscripts for the University of Pittsburgh Press. I was learning to edit, and it was not lost on me that twice during the period of my service the final judge of Pitt's United States Award Contest had recommended to the winning poet that a particular poem—obviously the judge's favorite—be moved to the beginning of the collection. From this I deduced that manuscripts were generally selected on the basis of one poem, and that it would behoove me to include every poem I'd ever written, since one could never know which might be a judge's favorite. On the slim chance that mine would be selected, I'd worry about ordering a tight collection later. When this happened and I insisted to Tom Lloyd, then the press director, who was editing my book, that it had to be cut in half for publication, he was dumbfounded, but finally agreed. I didn't learn until later that he had already sent the original "winning manuscript" to Thorp Menn so that he might prepare a timely review in the *Star*. Menn's piece, which appeared in the Sunday Book Section on the day before my reading in Kansas City, made mention of two poems—and quoted extensively from a third—that are not in the book. I was (and have remained) both embarrassed and amused.

Editing an anthology such as this one, which celebrates and pays tribute to a long-lived major book award while simultaneously serving as its elegy, has not been an easy endeavor. Sadly, I've discovered that three of the twenty-nine Devins winners were deceased before I began my work. I was more than a year into the editing before I was able to make contact with the last of the poets or the executors of their estates. As it happened, the most difficult for me was Edsel Ford. He'd published his poems widely during the fifties. I asked every poet I knew if they'd known him. Many had vague recollections, but nothing recent. I'd read the brief biography in his Devins book, which mentioned his being born in Alabama. I left my office one late fall afternoon resolved to go home and dial directory information in every Alabama city and town until I found him. I looked again at the bio statement. I'd neglected the short sentence about his moving to Arkansas. Immediately, I phoned Miller Williams at the University of Arkansas Press. Miller is a wonderful poet whose work I'd been introduced to while in graduate school. Lately he's become known as an editor and publisher, and by his appearance at a certain Presidential Inauguration. But I'd never made his acquaintance. Since one of his poetry volumes had been published by Missouri, I hoped he'd be sympathetic. I told him what I was doing. "I've been looking for months for a poet named Edsel Ford. Have you ever heard of him?" After a brief pause, and in a low tone, Miller replied, "Oh yes . . . he was my best friend . . ." And then he told me the story of their good times; about being graduate students together at Arkansas, about Ford's dying of a brain tumor as a young man, a mere two years after winning the Devins; how the Historical Society of Rogers, Arkansas, Edsel Ford's town, had a day in his honor a few years ago; how Miller had gone up there to read Ford's poems.

What's been most impressive—in addition to the kindness and energy of those I came into contact with while compiling this anthology—has been the eclecticism of the University of Missouri Press's poetry program over more than three decades. Certainly this is due to the democratic spirit of the judges (listed elsewhere in this volume), but also to the direction of Missouri's five press directors to date: William Peden, Robert Morris, Thomas Lloyd, Edward King, and Beverly Jarrett. If Robert Morris and Edward Devins in establishing their award had in mind anything like providing a counterpoint to the awards offered by the "Eastern Establishment" or groups on the "West Coast," which had, by the midsixties, begun to solidify its claim to being the "poetry capital," they surely succeeded. Nor did the Devins become a "Midwest" award. In its thirty years, the poets chosen resided in eighteen different states when they were selected: three were from New England, six from Middle Atlantic states, seven from the Midwest, five from the West, and eight from the South. One was from Missouri. Although some may argue the point, this seems to me to be a representation of the best for American poetry, and the best in American publishing. Ronald Wallace, in the introduction to his anthology *Vital Signs: Contemporary Poetry from the University Presses* (University of Wisconsin Press, 1989), claims convincingly that the lot of poetry publishing has, in the latter half of this century, fallen to the university presses: "Since 1960, university presses have published over 900 volumes, in recent years surpassing the trade publishers not only in quantity but in quality. . . . among younger writers particularly, university press poets have garnered the lion's share of such awards as the Lamont, the Guggenheim, and the Academy of American Poets. The Pulitzer Prize in Poetry has gone to university press books." A careful reading of these pages (as well as of Wallace's book, where he offers comparative lists of poetry titles and samplings from twenty-five university presses) will indicate that during this period Missouri's contribution to American poetry has been as great as anyone's; indeed, it has been much greater than most.

A brief word about the selection process: initially I wrote to all of the Devins winners asking them to send me the titles of the five poems that they felt were most representative. I wanted a sense of how they saw their work as opposed to my perceptions of it, but I indicated to them that, as editor, I would make the final selections. I read each of the twenty-nine books at least three times over a period of seven months. My goal was to select approximately nine finished pages from each work. Depending upon length, this resulted in the choice of between four and nine poems. As it happened, several of each poet's selections coincided with mine.

I wish to express my gratitude to the following individuals, whose aid and advice and, in some instances, technical expertise were instrumental in producing this anthology:

Beverly Jarrett for her guidance and patience; Jane Lago for her advice and brilliant copyediting; Tracy Martinez, Debbie Guilford, and Janice Smiley of the University of Missouri Press, upon whom I relied for basic information from the press archives on countless occasions; Margaret Sayers Peden, my telephone companion for two years, who provided leads in tracking down poets and sources, and her recollections of the history of the University of Missouri Press and its poetry program, as well as encouragement and a cheerful disposition on some very slow days;

Dan Jaffe, formerly of the University of Missouri–Kansas City and now of North Bay Village, Florida, who kindly shared information about the formulation of The Devins Award and the Kansas City Poetry Contests; Mary Ellen Buck and James McKinley of the University of Missouri–Kansas City; Jennifer Dalton of the *Kansas City Star;*

Miller Williams, Stanley Moss, George Garrett, Dale Cushner, Judy Longley, Catherine Bennett-Garrigan, and Elizabeth M. Bennett for helping me to locate various poets or their representatives;

Cynthia Lamb of Carnegie Mellon University Press

for her skill at transcribing, and for reading, commenting on, and formatting the manusript; John Biggs, undergraduate intern with Carnegie Mellon University Press for, among other of his talents, livening up the joint; Aron Schmid, Cynthia Davis, Paula Pfleiger, Brian Miles, Chris Muenzer, Kris Tomasette, David Oleszkiewicz, and, especially, Kristen Grasso, student FDSL User Consultants at Carnegie Mellon University; and, finally, to the Devins Award winners themselves for their prompt responses to my requests; but mostly for their beautiful poems.

Gerald Costanzo
Harwich, Massachusetts

Nancy Sullivan

The History of the World as Pictures

1965

Nancy Sullivan's additional collections of poetry are *To My Body* (Hellcoal Press) and *Telling It* (Godine). She has edited three anthologies for Doubleday, *The Treasuries of American Poetry*, *American Short Stories*, and *English Short Stories*, all recently reissued under the imprint of Barnes and Noble. She lives in West Kingston, Rhode Island.

The History of the World as Pictures

The poem about the history of the world
As pictures will be in pieces like the history
Of that world and like those pictures
Each separate upon a wall in separate places.
Lined up they may be the meaning of the world
Or they may be the only world with meaning.

Prehistoric Cave Painting of a Bison

Perhaps it was being inside of something
That caused them to render it outside
By scrawling great beasts in screams
Of rust and black over the walls of the cave.
Perhaps it was the visitation of an idea,
An event so powerful
As to turn them into men.

The bison is taut inside the readiness
Of its fur. It has no dimensions
Because it is already huge. Miniature
Black men resembling the matches
No one yet knows about cast needles
At the beast that is as large as Africa.
What it must have been like to scramble
In out of a rain to discover not only
The sensation of dryness, but a place
That had been visited by a god.

Las Meniñas by Velazquez (1656)

The dwarfs dominate, at least theatrically.
The little princess near the center, illuminated
In her petulant reluctance to pose for yet
Another portrait illustrates an idea of order,

Not the governing parents, the mother and the father,
Philip IV and Mariana of Austria, mere reflections
In the distant mirror in the far places of the paint.
The commissioned artist accepts a royal order
Although he alone governs this pigment territory
Where dwarfs rule and ugliness flowers to virtue.

We look into the picture to watch a situation,
Into a tall room in the Alcazar hung with copies of
        Rubens.
The Infanta Doña Margarita doesn't want to pose.
She is five years old and has had enough of paint.
But forces are at work here: the perspective
That holds the room together and holds the Rubens
On to the painted walls. There are triangles
Of people whose duties are enormous, eleven in all.
Velazquez must pain, the ladies-in-waiting,
Las meniñas, must cajole and pass some chocolate
To the princess. The king and queen must
Be that, but here without a single power.
The man going up the steps must go up them.
In the right hand corner, the dwarf Nicolasito
Is stepping on the dog. Another, Maribarbola,
Stares out of her massive face to tell a royal story.

Her brief finery is the somber opposite of little
Margarita's bright and golden style. She rules
No empire nor ever will, but here she dominates the
        mind.

Beauty, a dog, and this wizened female
So ugly, so sad, so sufficient to this scene
As to make you wonder at the governments of men.
How detached the painter's glance now that he has
Put everyone in his place and upset the candor of Spain.

Number 1 by Jackson Pollock (1948)

No name but a number.
Trickles and valleys of paint
Devise this maze
Into a game of Monopoly
Without any bank. Into
A linoleum on the floor
In a dream. Into
Murals inside of the mind.
No similes here. Nothing
But paint. Such purity
Taxes the poem that speaks
Still of something in a place
Or at a time.
How to realize his question
Let alone his answer?

Money

The rich are important to a culture.
They and what they had are all that's left
Once the buildings topple and the people
Arrange themselves for archaeology.
Gauge a people by its rich.
All the Chippendale and artifacts
Of Williamsburg are early America
To me, not those stinking stowaways
Vomiting their way to Massachusetts.

So it was in Greece and earlier in Babylonia.
The poor are merely figures on parade.
They march along the walls of the tomb of a rich man.
The whole place is a poorhouse where weaver and
        brewer
Cart this and that to there for the man who has preserved
Their thin selves and their endless little skills.

In the Fields

The green antennae of the hedges sharpen into sticks.
The crusty Fall explodes its colors.
The trees strew rusty ruins on the lawn.
This house is stiff against the simple field.
Barbed wire divides the lawn, from the unmoved land.
The smell of the place is something gold.

In the fields the cows, season after season,
Swirl those wigged swatters round their rumps,
Metronomes clocking the small annoyances of Eden.

Besides them, what is in these empty places?
What so tough and soothing there
As that salt block on a cow's rough tongue?
Everything that has been so forever.
The low bleat of the world began in ferny spaces.
And when it ends in crater scooped out
Of the sand as on a moon gone out,
This landscape, already what it never was,
Will wear its own memory,
A place that needs no snow to sweeten itself to virtue;
This morning, the field is pale with peace.

The House by the Sea

The dining room laps over the edge,
A napkin over the rock.
Tilted toward Block Island
The tip of lawn slopes, leaps
In gulls of green
From here, the dark bedroom,
Where I have caught the moon
Mimicking birds on the water.
Once when the windows were very clean
I watched Eldorado map out

Of the sea to ebb into the parlor—
Massive, sandy, a mirage on the rug.
Only Noah all that time in the wooden ark
Dribbling porter over the waters of the world
Understood how the looking out encloses you.

What Time?

The wheel, the plow
happened,
possibly on a Friday.
Events happen.
They do not begin.

That old woman
thumping down the road
happens along.
She happens to me,
and I am as though
it rained forever.

He Has No Personal Life

Pedaling down the primitive road,
Pushing, pumping in a whiz,
He has no personal life.
The trees mesh above, so underneath
Night and day splatter on the ground
Shaping a dapple tent over the cruising man.
Under his hat, so camouflaged,
He merges with the road to color with the land.
Such signals in an hour: mailbox,
Fence, cow, tractor, bicycle with man
Flick onto the retina's clean spaces.

As the pattern from the trees tells
Nothing for a page, so this cycling man
Enters the mind as sun might.
He has no personal life.

Saul Touster

Still Lives and Other Lives

1966

Born in 1925 in Brooklyn, Saul Touster was educated
at Harvard and served in the Navy during World
War II. He received his law degree and practiced
law before entering university teaching in 1955. He
has since retired and lives in Boston, where he
continues to write poetry.

Green Apple: Still Life I

A thing such as this is
can't contain more of itself
than its seed can

and yet by late afternoon
something else, something entirely other
than the green apple
 joins it on the table
and gives it support.

Maybe it's the blue background
darkening or a gesture that favors
roundness over weight.
Still, it's the right weight
in the hand, and cold,
and sets the teeth
on edge.

Green Apple: Still Life II

Green grows the apple
in the real blue air
blowing the air
from the apple's sheen
holding together
even the stem
the lemons in the distance.

As if the stillness weren't enough.

Green grows the core
and the shadow of the core
wearing the shape of an apple.

Green Apple: Still Life III

What will come of it
all that light
the light of the lemons
the three pale suns?

To reveal a few consistencies
to make known an intention
to find a place

it clears the air
and settles on the apple's green skin
the apple's green and glazed skin

and then the dark resemblances begin.

Kafka's Funeral

The mother,
who should never have lived
to bury a son,
could not believe
she had become the dead man's child.
She wept like a child.
The father,
who should have given the boy a break
by dying first,
could not believe
this was the letter his son sent.
He kept in his mind
an early version
unbelievably innocent.
The betrothed could not believe
this was the bridal bed.
And the friends who came

could not believe
it was June
when tree follows tree in flower
and the frog jumps like the frog.

Lunch Hour Idyll

Budding iris in April—
in the shadow of Trinity Church
where Wall Street begins
among stones and grass
and historic prisoners of grass.
Sandwiched between the hours
the church clock races
from graveyard to river,
the iris takes its tear-shape time.
After a long winter
the office girls sun themselves—
their coats open,
their eyes closed.

Vision

I have seen a funeral
    cut in two
        by a red light

squirming
    in the bad blood
        of civic horns,

and then the sirens
    joined the severed parts
        and howled them

to the rim of the
   grave. A policeman
      removing

his hat & gloves
   and shaking hands
      with the man in charge

receives a ten spot
   in the palm
      solemn as communion.

I was silent,
   blinded
      by his white teeth.

Salo the Artist
—*for Roland Wise*

i. His family life

"Keeper of the snakehouse!"
Cry out his in-laws
through the skylight.
"Look at his shoes—
spotted by the droppings of a career!"
He voids them by an act of concentration,
but they break through
the skylight
raining
slivers upon him.
At his feet, they whine
amidst the faecal paint and critic-money
rushing from their wounds.

ii. *His model cuts both ways*

There is a certain justice
to her breasts he would point up
at the expense of her thighs.
But she who's never satisfied
carries her plight
on the slope of the shoulder
he is oblivious to.
He munches on a cheese.
She stares through the skylight.
"The clouds make pictures," she says.
He is a cloud.
What can you expect
of a man trying to do justice
to breasts which are, in the end,
not his? She disturbs the peace.
Madonna of the cheese!
He would draw blood
every time.

v. *Even the aesthetics may be relevant*

In the Salon des Refusés
the world is,
the eye recruits passions
the mind spends
and spreads them on the grass in quivering light.
Everything is made new!
except the irreducible old
wavelengths: landscapes
as bare as flesh darken
and crack. X-rayed
in 400 years the canvas shows
a lesion of the left lung.

Nancy Willard

Skin of Grace

1967

Nancy Willard resides in Poughkeepsie, New York. Her most recent collections of poetry include *Water Walker* (Knopf) and *Among Angels*, a correspondence in poetry with Jane Yolen (Harcourt Brace).

Victory Garden

We planted our garden small.
After dinner my mother and I

tidied the beans, watching the apples fall,
while the radio, hid in a melon pile,

counted the deaths in trenches and fields.
The corn tall as my brother, whose smile

I can hardly remember, pushed out green hands
to my mother like awaited friends.

When he died, she hid in the tall sheaves.
They too were cut down, a battalion

of comforters, yet the next years the leaves
came again. How do such things survive?

cried my mother. We ploughed our grief
under the stubble alive

and tried to imagine that fields in France,
very yellow and empty now, the stalks

of wheat pushing quietly out of the earth,
those witnesses and quiet conquerors.

Transcript, 1848

I think none of us knew her; yet everyone
knew the girl from Amherst, young for her class,
dark hair severely parted, attendance
somewhat irregular, for which
she came, reserved and sullen, to my office.

When she lifted her head, you saw the eyes
of a surgeon parsing your spirit. Once a law

student arrived asking for Miss Dickinson, and she,
sprigged and awkward, served tea; I was a bit
astonished, thinking she had no one. Curling
her lip slightly, she read the class
her essay on Pope, brilliant and strange,
into which she dissolved like a shower of sparks,
In chapel, she knelt with her hands clenched

rather than folded. The gentleman caller
did not come again; "I had a friend who taught
me Immortality, but venturing too near,
himself, he never returned."
During the retreat for penitents,
I looked out and saw her,
cutting across the forbidden grass,

making as usual her own path.
Prayers in her mouth crumbled to clay;
Christ and the Trinity might have been
the jam pot, the butter on
the table, a good book. During a reprimand
she stared angrily, pitifully out at flowers.
Standing at my door, waiting to see me,

not knocking, but listening for the sound of
my breath on the other side, she seemed
—how shall I call her?—ghostly, waking to
terror in the grey chill of the class
and the patient responses of pupils dozing,
while she, flayed by the new space, felt the air
nailing her down, then the final closing.

Legend

There's a forest in Sweden that flowers
on Christmas night. You'll find berries,
same as in ours, says the farmer who hasn't
seen it but whose mother saw it once.

That was in Småland. Fifty miles north
an old man who paints churches saw
the same forest, though he never walks
farther than his farthest field,

where the wood starts again, everywhere silent.
It was all blossoms and strange birds, he says.
He didn't remember their names though he knew
they'd met before, perhaps at midsummer

in sight of his own pasture, over the ashes
where his neighbor's children danced
the whole light long. To enter your own life
as if you knew nothing is the root

of miracles; to be walking among the dead
farms hunched in snow, the sheds and extinct
gardens and glancing up, to see in a far
window flowers hang like desire

on the dark, where the farmer's wife
and her cats are eating a lonely supper.
Then—not to know this place but the legend,
breaking the snow with ferns and dogwood and wild
        scent.

The messengers of grace are ignorant.

The Insects

They pass like a warning of snow,
   the dragonfly, mother of millions,
the scarab, the shepherd spider,
   the bee. Our boundaries break
on their jeweled eyes,
   blind as reflectors.
The black beetle
   under the microscope wears the
blue of Chartres. The armored
   mantis, a tank in clover,
folds its wings like a flawless
   inlay of wood, over and over.

"There is something about insects
   that does not belong to the habits
of our globe," said Maeterlinck,
   touching the slick
upholstery of the spider,
   the watchspring and cunning
tongue of the butterfly, blown out
   like a paper bugle. Their humming
warns us of sickness, their silence
   of honey and frost. Asleep
in clapboards and rafters,
   their bodies keep

the cost of our apples and wool.
   A hand smashes their wings,
tearing the veined
   landscape of winter trees.
In the slow oozing of our days
   who can avoid remembering
their silken tents on the air,
   the spiders wearing their eggs
like pearls, born on muscles
   of silk, the pulse of a rose, baiting

the moth that lives for three hours,
  lives only for mating?

Under a burning glass, the creature
  we understood disappears. The dragonfly
is a hawk, the roach
  cocks his enormous legs at your acre,
eyes like turrets piercing
  eons of chitin and shale. Drummers
under the earth, the cicadas
  have waited for seventeen summers
to break their shell,
  shape of your oldest fear
of a first world
  of monsters. We are not here.

In the Hospital of the Holy Physician

In the hospital of the holy physician, I hear
no voices in the waiting room.
No nurses with needles take my name
or jab the beat of my harlequin fear,
    my jewel-in-the-heart
    that tried so long
    to make my life an art.

In the hospital of the holy physician I come
wearing the shape of sin
like a love-child under my skin.
The voices clotting my blood go numb.
    I do not sleep, I see
    rooms break like bones
    to set me free.

In the hospital of the holy physician, I move
toward the scalpel judiciously hurled
at my brain till healing has pearled
a pilgrimage on each rotten groove,

shining and clear.
In the pulse of my ruin
I make my cure.

The Healers
—from the print by Helen Siegl

Under your foot at dusk, smell
the compassionate herbs. Their being

is being broken for our need.
Periwinkle, joy of the ground

"maketh a meek stomach and a good heart."
Caraway in comfits, fennel and seed

of vervain, the simples of grace,
heal us of witchcraft and wagging teeth.

Comforters of the aged and blind,
you make the sinner chaste.

Carried like a staff, you open the dark.
Watchman, what of the night? And you

the servant whose waiting we hardly see:
I am here. Take me.

The Church

If the walls are whitewashed clean, I hope
that under the show of purity I can find
a mural of monkeys pressing wine,
that below the candles on the choir stall

someone has carved a dancing bear or a boy
riding a wild boar.

The man who makes the dragon under the
saint's feet must know the dragon is

beautiful. And therefore, on the altar,
the Bible will rest on the back of a griffin
to remind you that the beast is present
in every birth.

You shall not exclude them from the communion
of saints and men. If the roof is plain
put a cock on the steeple; you shall not
exclude them from your marriages.

Skin of Grace

It will have the color of clod,
    the smell of fennel, the slow shape

of desire and slick of otter.
    In a place burning with hate

it will heal like clearest water.
    A crowd of clocks clacking together

makes no time but a sound like streams
    where deer drinking conquer the armed man

by their vast astonishment and silence.
    It is a meeting he does not expect.

Who can command this coming?
    Out of the dark rafters, the skeletal shed,

It spreads like a blossoming field, raises
    a field forgotten, forgiving, to quicken and taste,

O see the healing, the linnets, the spinning worm,
    the flash and pivot of creatures living
        under the skin of grace.

Edsel Ford

Looking for Shiloh

1968

Born in Alabama, Edsel Ford resided in Rogers,
Arkansas. He received a B.A. in English from the
University of Arkansas, Fayetteville, in 1952. While
an undergraduate he published a chapbook of
poems entitled *A Stallion's Nest*. Mr. Ford served for
two years in the United States Army. He died of a
brain tumor in 1970 at the age of forty-one.

Contingent

In water as in wind we shape
Our arms around familiar bodies.
Beds know the way we are;
Chairs turn to living shells.

The runner finds earth
First fact of his running;
The medium of the flier
Is air, his coexistent.

Man the Upright is a lie.
Something is always there
To cradle him: water,
Earth, fire, or air.

Low Tide at Fire Island

It is ourselves we mourn when tides recede
To leave our bleached bones balanced on the ripples
Of sand and foam. We are the only cripples
In evidence; all other things are freed
By ebb and flow. In our insatiable greed
We tied the farmhouse down, the crib, the stables,
The rickrack fence, the doghouse, picnic tables . . .
Even the wind's denied the tethered steed.
So these are our bones, left from other summers.
We grieve among them, choosing what we will
To put ourselves together from the grave;
But the tide departs, erasing half the numbers,
And, uninstructed, we have not the skill
To make us whole with these few parts we have.

White River Float

Translating summer into another tongue,
The boat lisps through the cold emerald
Water, through the onyx deeps and the crystal riffles,
Spinning late fallen leaves into yellow chapters
And red oak volumes.

The thermal-knit fisherman flicks ice from his line,
Casting and reeling from bank to boat.
Somewhere a bass is lurking; somewhere a jack
Noses a pebbled recollection of the sporting summer.

Here the long fingers of willows write on the water;
Here the log deciphers the cryptic pool;
The wintering river glosses its margins with meaning.
High on a naked hill the symbolic staccato
Of a yellowhammer shatters the frozen hush.

It has been a long time since the last geese flew.
It will be a long time before they fly again.
But this boat moves north, for the river runs that way:
Summer or winter, this river runs north.

And the fingers of the willows write on the water.

Foreword for a Second Edition

Duned in the doom of his impeccable grave
My uncle never guessed how in demand
Would be his letters from the western land
Where he had gone for his health, that rave on rave
Would squander his unlearned assets of love
For his dear older brother left to read
The anguish in these lines, nor that our greed
Could dig him up, though he were dead enough.

Had this insatiable hunger knocked on doors
Sooner by forty years, if those who throw
Three dollars down for his incredible verse
Had done it earlier, he would on sunlit shores
Live now who died in San Antonio
And came home wreathed in garlands, in a hearse.

The Image of Desire

We never knew when next the fox might strike,
But many a dark night lying in the loft
Straining our ears to catch the swift, the soft,
The cunning coming of him or his like,
We held a fortress as men hold a wake:
Silent and grim, bound to a solemn task
Which wasn't interrupted even to ask
The time; our boyhood honor was at stake.
And often when the cock crew, shaking fire
Out of the morning and the misty mow,
We stayed on, staring, hard put to leave off,
Lest in the wood the image of desire
Spring up behind us yapping, although now
We know we've kept this vigil long enough.

Turning Loose

Once as I clung
To the arm of my father
I hung
In the water.

How deep was too deep
I could not fathom:
His white legs kept
An easy rhythm.

Then down to my chin
And up from my doubt
He let me in,
He let me out.

And when at length
He let me free
I swam with strength
Of two or three.

But he went down
All green and gold.
I watched him drown.
And then grow old.

About Grampa, Who Died Poor

My grandfather in his once-Spenserian hand
Cribbed by the cold which scotched his ancient bones
Wrote two-cent postcards out of Dixieland
To twenty kin and near-kin, Smith and Jones
And several mixed up of a foreign name,
Saying *Now I am free, I might arrange a trip* . . .
Ready to travel before the postman came:
Clothes in a parcel, medicines in a grip.
But those who answered said they had the flu,
Or were about to move, or *Maybe later*;
And he, having nothing nothing whatever to do,
Got too old even for the elevator,
Much less the train—lamenting most, no doubt,
The forty cents it took to feel them out.

Perspectives

At twenty-one
I was pursued
By a wall of flame
In a scarlet wood;

But I escaped.
Now I inquire
At every door
"A little fire?"

Lines for the First Day

Suddenly the world depends on you. The wall
Hangs from your picture holding its breath
As if, were your likeness moved, it might fall
Upon the air and the useless floor beneath.
Waking, the day awaits to hear the tick
Of you before continuing its rise.
All that was dead is suddenly somehow quick
To stir: dogs, milk trucks, and other liberties.
And I, dying all night lest you be gone
In dream or real with some dark charioteer
When I should wake, myself leap up like dawn
To feel you stirring—oh alive! alive!

All things assume their native postures. I've
Been reprieved, thank God!—and you're still here.

John Calvin Rezmerski

Held for Questioning

1969

John Calvin Rezmerski, writer-in-residence at
Gustavus Adolphus College, has been an editor,
scriptwriter, political speechwriter, magician, story-
teller, cook, typesetter, and school board member.
His additional collections of poems include *An
American Gallery*, published by Three Rivers Press.
Mr. Rezmerski is a resident of Eagle Lake, Minne-
sota.

Supplement to an Ethic

A man should love his work,
even if he is a soldier.
He should sing while loading and firing
and rejoice in a good hit.
If the bayonet is a thorn,
he should be the rose.
This is a sensible, practical love,
the kind that exists between fish.
Love will kill a king,
love includes the teeth,
love deceives the palate.
And work well done
deserves a man and his love.

Animism II

This bench is alive.
My father made it.
The table is dead;
we bought it that way
to put things on.
I have a candle.
It lives,
when somebody lights it.

Nobody lights the sun
but it is alive too,
because nobody buys it.

My father told me
some people buy other people.
Somebody should go light them.
People are not
to put things on.

American Motives

Do not defile me:
the slogan we shout
from inside statues.
Our bodies are transparent enough
to look out of;
only the animals can see in.
That is the right of holiness
and we know it.
We want to be werewolves,
long teeth prowling
on innocent feet.
We worship our own lives;
that is why we disperse the congregations of pigeons.
That is why.

Courtship and Conquest

So I told her what I wanted
and bang, across the face.
If that's the kind
I thought she was,
I could leave—now.
Shocked, utterly shocked.
How could I?
Never mind the kisses,
between friends;
I should have
my hands lopped off
like a long-ago thief.
She was a cat
with her tail trod on;
at my car she grabbed my arm,
said she loved me, don't go.
It was the same thing

every time,
all the way to the altar.

A Posteriori

Removing your ornaments
you make me predict things:
someday you will teach me concupiscence.
Then you will want
to carry my eyes around in your purse,
letting them out only behind doors.
Religion is mixed up in this,
you and your inquisition.
But the sin is only gluttony:
me demanding you demanding
the chance to be my widow.

Pragmatism

1.   Say I'm a builder.
        It's October,
        a strange city.
        I'm on the street
        watching the lights go off and on.
        The people are leaping from rooftops.
        I'll have to stop building.

2.   I have watched the lights
        of uninhabited towns,
        sent postcards
        to the deadletter office,
        inquiring about jobs.
        Sometimes, walking back and forth from the
            mailbox,
        I get a stone in my shoe.

I hate addresses,
but keep writing.

3.   I should pick up my hammer,
breathe like I used to,
slap boards together
wherever they fit.
I could absolve myself
by ignoring the blueprints
I would shout, My buildings!
Come see!
And people would come
and not jump
for lack of a plan.

Guest of Honor

A man realized he was dead,
told them No
and meant it.
A hundred percent dead,
wanted to be remembered.
He was a hundred percent
gone out of his shoes for good.

Eternity will have to go on without me,
he said.
Having faith in rumors
about man-eating worms,
he tried to screw himself back into his body.

It is my personal conveyance,
he said.
It is my heritage,
he said,
I live by it,

I have a right to keep it,
I brought it here with me.

We all think we are visitors
from someplace important.
So.

Fossil

Someday I may be found hardened
between layers of rock
keeping a vigil over a dead river.
Dynamite will free me,
make room for a factory,
a munitions plant.
I will be stored
in the back room of a museum.
Me, who wanted
to guard the world
against earthquakes and insults.

Fall Morning

Standing in the fog by the highway,
I can call the passing trucks ships;
standing in the fog, alone,
nobody has to believe me.

John Bennett

The Struck Leviathan: Poems on *Moby Dick*

1970

John Bennett was born March 20, 1920, in Pittsfield, Massachusetts, and was raised in Tilton, New Hampshire. He received his B.A. from Oberlin College in 1947 and his M.A. and Ph.D. degrees from the University of Wisconsin in 1950 and 1956. During his career he taught at Indiana University, Beloit College, Rockford College, and, for many years, at St. Norbert College. He died on November 30, 1991.

Ishmael: Loomings, Christmas Day, Late

The *Pequod's* bows, vindictive, blunt with doom,
appareled with the jawbones of dead whales,
drove eyeless eastward into her sea room.
She caught the night wind in her thrumming sails
then slanted southward on the vague sea trails

far past Nantucket where the hungry dark
devoured the circles of eternity,
and Ahab braced himself on his stumped mark
to schism blankness into agony
and prove him human to the alien sea.

Father Mapple: On the Abyss of the Godhead

Sweet Isaac, helpless near the bush,
felt flame start wildly on his skin:
God took that flame and cast it round
the greenleaf bush and hotly in
to save old Abraham from sin.

And then the Ram, the Holy Ram,
became Child's Holy Surrogate:
He burned within the burning bush
and made both God and Man elate
that They were Christ's Beginning State.

Ishmael: In the Crow's Nest

At the ship's zenith close to heaven's depth,
the heavy boom of the bows comes faintly up
then fades through thin hysterias of wind
that mewl along the spars.
                              I cling white-knuckled here.

Behind my eyes, coiled mysteries of height
beckon the sea to circles at my feet
$\qquad\qquad\qquad$ or I
hang like a pendulum, dropped from the ship's deep
$\qquad$ root
down through the swing of the sky.
$\qquad\qquad\qquad\qquad\qquad$ I cling hard! hard!
to snaking lines lest I should slip and fall
straight upward through the empyrean clouds
or downward through the empyrean waves.

A German trap! A dreadful subtlety!

I call it losing self. I call it Death:
the Noumenon that Plato praised until
he drowned in honied cisterns of the mind.

I loose one hand, forcing the muscle and bone,
then gear me to the motion of this task
and live within my skin's circumference.

Ahab: At His Cabin Window, Midnight

This shackling cube! caged concentrate of space
borne rigidly above the swirling tides
that suck along the strakes and rudderpost!
Cribbed in this darkly pitching coffin, I
can watch my mind plumb through immensities,
through the chill malice of a universe
that Starbuck might no sooner learn to fear
than he did mother's milk!
$\qquad\qquad\qquad\qquad$ Poor mooncalf! grown
brawny as oak, but in his ultimates
as flimsy as some village natural
that cucks and coos over an autumn leaf,
mistaking scarlet for a sign of joy!

I know what he can never dare to know:
by my hurt driven hard, I ram the voids,
denying them by ramming through them, thus!
and chart a godlike course.
                              No single sea
can float the keelson of my great intent:
the winds that rip that wavecurve into spume
are subject to my sail; and all the stars
that crack the firmament with frozen light
are merely points upon the private chart
that leads me circling back to my whole self!

Bulkington: **The Struck Leviathan**

Like stoats that dare their own death if they hope
to sip at murdered veins, the whaleboats crept
with cunning lust across the heave to slope
where sea and air thrust flowing alternates.

Among the plankton sun tides where he slept,
the vivid lances woke the dreaming beast
to lunge and agony. His great flukes swept
a tumbled sea through roils to crimson yeast.
The iron rived his heart with alien gates
while overhead the mindless sea birds danced
a phantom woe upon the spinning air.

Oh! mourn the gallied whale whose death advanced
as he lay dreaming in his sunny lair!

Ishmael: **The Pod**

Under soft sunlight
on the glinting tides
the gentle sea beasts roll
in love or loving play.

Those children of salt time—
those bulls whose greatly muscled sex
would cause the Bull to stare,
those cows whose filling wombs make birth
the absolute of love,
those calves whose innocence hurls them
through tides of hugest joy—
those tons of flesh are gentle as the kiss
that other lovers give.

The halcyon sea and its great beasts are one:
God's holy purpose, single, multiform,
defines a joyous image of itself.

Ahab: **Near the Mainmast, Sunrise**

Into this madman horror of the sun
how many men crawl forth reluctant now
from the grey swamps of sleep and dress themselves
in clothes that stink with mortal yesterdays ?

Cursed endless *batter! batter!* wind and wave!
bows crashing down, green water surging up,
and the long, whining dip of mast and spar!

Who truly listens on this ship? Who hears?
Across the fronts of heaven, silence grows
between the muted thunder of old suns
like some enormous cancer;
                                        here, the sea
roars out its manic scansion, pauses, beats,
lifts to crescendo scream, and then drops down
through seething voids that drain my outraged heart
of its warm rhythms.

                    Soon ! Soon! Oh! Soon!
that blunt-faced phantom from the shrouded depths,

that damned razeeing bastard devil brute
whose rending jaw cut coldly at my quick
will rise to meet me on the upper seas!
In what last tide or precinct of my course
will he breach forth to learn that I can kill?
No matter where he hides, no matter where!
I'll chase him out across the compass rose,
through every strait and passage of the sea!
I'll chase him round the Maelstrom's triple lip
and round the brimming flames of Hell itself
until my lance drives down through his heart's root!

Come, Moby Dick! My compliments to ye!
My compliments, my very best to ye!
I bear a gift of tempered steel whose edge,
baptized with blood almost as wild as yours,
will force ye to attend me when we meet
and grave sweet lessons on your sullen heart!

Come, Moby Dick! Come, Moby Dick! Come! Come!

Ishmael: **Death of Ahab**

Flesh-borne in whale, the world's blind windigoes
leapt forth to murder Ahab
                              AND! the sea,
grown prodigal with many coral dooms,
fell back from vortex into liturgy:
            Men and their Final Angel meet
            on curving wave, on level street:
                  Timor mortis conturbat eos.

On far green lands, the heavy cities rust
in careless sunlight
                        AND! beneath carved stones,
through crazy scatters of enormous dark,
the frightened dreamers hide unhinging bones:

Men and their Final Angel soon
meet in the dying afternoon:
Timor mortis conturbat eos.

Ishmael: 'Pequod' Down

After the whaleblow, atilt as in windcurve
then
poised on the round lip of vortex and shatter
then
the *Pequod* foundered in deep skirl of downpitch.

All of her bright men, caged in the maelstrom,
blossomed like flowers. And Tashtego opened
sunward his petals of laughter.

Sea wind whine, a curlew piping.
Fiercely the manforms broke dark waves to silver
and death cries were trumpets, were split-echo coral.

Henry Carlile

The Rough-Hewn Table

1971

Henry Carlile has published two additional poetry collections, *Running Lights* and *Rain*. His honors include grants from the National Endowment for the Arts, the Ingram Merrill Foundation, and the Oregon Arts Commission, two Pushcart Prizes, and *Crazyhorse* magazine's 1988 poetry award.

Grandmother

No one remembered when she first discovered God.
Her conversion was sudden as a slammed door.
Outside, my grandfather beat the doorjamb with his fist,
But she, God-furious, would not relent.
Shut up like an oyster on a speck of dirt
She praised God in her bedclothes,
Read the Bible like a French novel,
And dreamed each night of Christ the Saviour,
The lightning bolt of revelation forking at her
From the black cloud of her Bible,
And the godhead stirring inside her like a sick sea.

Overnight her skirts grew longer and her temper shorter,
The black buttons on her boots crept higher and higher
On legs that had never seen the light.
Whenever she rode the cable car downtown
She pulled her bonnet tight around her ears
To let no evil word hiss through,
Her eyes magnified by scripture,
Split by the seeing lens and reading lens
Which could never look together,
Beholders of two worlds: one black and one white,
Negative, censored, and unprintable,
A damned world bleached of color.

Stern as an iron stove
She drove her children off to church,
Beat their bottoms with a willow
To make them kneel like thirteen sinful sheep,
Recalcitrant, flagellant, bleating at the altar,
Pinched upright in their pews,
Reciting alphabets of sin while the preacher,
A red-faced Russian with a beard as black as God,
Gospeled from the pulpit
And the congregation flapped their tongues,
Prophesying improbable forgiveness.

But nothing ever was:
The family scattered out like rabbits
From the sawed-off shotgun of the true faith
While Grandmother rocked in the cradle of belief,
Reading and praying, reading and praying,
Copying scriptures on tiny scraps of paper
That peeped like mice or children
From every nook and cranny of the old house:
From cookie jars and table drawers and kitchen
       cupboards—
Even from the Bible itself, marsupial with
       misconceptions,
Threatening every minute to explode,
Until one day her heart did,
And we hunkered in the shadow of her death,
A bad-luck come-to-nothing family
Wrong since genesis.

Three for the Predators

At midnight on the riverbank,
burglars prowl sly-whiskered,
pilfering from the shallows
clams shut up like banks on Sunday,
quick-pincered crayfish,
snails coiled springtight
into a country of themselves,
fastidious fast fingers that probe,
find everything rock-bottom,
safe for those who touch
with a safecracker's old know-how.

High in the hemlock
eyes like two August moons blink down,
broad wings launch out suddenly
extending hooks to grapple in the depths
of air, of snow, for timider lives

of lesser consequence,
which know no acquittal
but that fine instinctual alacrity
of the hunted.

In the green world we carry with us
like a secret illness from a city
we've escaped,
know, too, the shadow suspended in green space,
the long head in which the flat eyes
tip like platters,
the two red crescent moons at the throat,
the long mouth's sinister grin,
and the chain-marked, snakelike body
waiting to swallow
anything that moves.

The Job

At one point he comes simply to ask, why bother?
Wearing your look, speaking your speech,
Which of course are unknown to you,
He confronts you like an old friend, someone to trust.
When you complain, he smiles patient as father.
He sees into your deepest self, exposing the irrational
Motives for all your behavior, mildly explaining
In language even a simpleton might understand
Why if you don't live in the right place, if your name
Has so far as anyone can tell no right recognizable
Ethnic roots, if you know no one who can do you
A favor, you can be ignored forever because
So far as anyone who has anything whatsoever
To do with anything important happens to be
Concerned you don't exist except as a postmark,
Provincial, primitive, quaint, any one of a dozen or so
Epithets to be dropped at any gathering at which
Fashionable topics are exchanged like make-believe

Banknotes in a game of chance.
                              At which time
He remarks it's past midnight, it's time
He was going and goodbye and please call
It was nice seeing you again and leaves
At which point you remove the cotton from your ears
And return to that unfinished perfectly useless
        whatever-
It-was-you-were-about-to-do-before-he-called which lies
Where you left it, impossible, urgent and necessary
On the rough-hewn table lost among mountains and
        waterfalls.

Three Monuments

At Teddy Roosevelt's statue
grandfathers gather to talk
war, leaning on canes
in the easy attitudes
of mountain men propped up
on muskets.
                The shadow of
Teddy Roosevelt's sword
falls across their feet.

As the cannon aims into
a blank river fog,
the flagstaff's empty halyard
bangs in a cold wind.

The mast of the *Oregon*
commemorates its absence
and the old ironclad
excuse of privilege.

Georgic from Henry's Lake
—Henry's Lake, Idaho

It is like fishing for a line of poetry,
only in this case you already have the line
and the leader tied in diminishing lengths and strengths
and finished with the finest tippet.
The fly should be one of your own creation since
art is important here and the means of taking your trout
are as important as the end.

And, as in oratory, the presentation must be exact
lest you offend your audience, among whom the oldest
are invariably the wisest.
A line delivered too hastily will fall heavily,
driving away all but the most inexperienced and naive.
Conversely, too casual an approach never reaches
its objective and may wind up in your head
or in a heap at your feet.
Sure coordination of the hand, eye and a
perfect sense of time are essential.
And finally, it helps to have balance.
This last is most important, for unless a universal
equanimity is created and sustained, any force will
       provoke
a counterforce to defeat you.

The object in this case is to roll the line
with enough impetus and finesse to duplicate nature,
so that the fly, mimicking its spent natural counterpart,
comes lightly and buoyantly to rest,
close enough to attract the attention of your quarry
but not so close as to frighten it.

If in addition to this you are patient,
content to endure long hours of painful reflection,
a shadow may rise swifter than thought
to shatter the blandest surface.

For ideas and trout strike when
least expected and are gone before we have grasped
      them.

But supposing for once you have done everything right,
and the barb is set,
the line must never be too tight lest the leader break
or the hook straighten.
On the other hand, if it is too slack the trout
may throw the fly on the first jump
or hang the line on a hidden snag.
As soon as possible you should retrieve all loose line,
especially if the fish runs toward you, playing it directly
from the reel, keeping the tackle at the proper angle
to avoid breaking it or using up its backbone,
thus losing all resilience
and in all likelihood the fish as well.
It will take at least this much skill and a little luck
to subdue your adversary
and much more self-discipline after it is safely landed
to let it go.

Endurances

A mountain climber turned evangelist confesses,
"Hanging on a face, I think like a fly.
The slightest error will kill.
And when I'm so close to death
suddenly I think of life.
The lichen in the crevices burns
with a pale green flame,
I think with my fingertips and toes,
no ideas but what I see and touch.
I think of Lot's wife and don't look back."

A sociologist tells of a soldier
squatting by the roadside after an ambush

in which two of his friends had been killed,
weeping, rapt over the simple beauty of a flower,
the meaning of which was surely lost
on the objective detachment of the unbiased observer
who could but wonder at the absurd juxtaposition,
the blood in the ditches and the blood-red flower.

I have heard a racing driver tell of hurling his
life through sudden turns so fast
he lost himself in stillness,
became a cipher on the tachometer,
the blurred shape of a bird in a dream of trees.

And diving we find rapture in the depths,
when perceiving our immortality we tear off masks
and glide naked and glistening to our deaths.

Jonathan Holden

Design for a House

1972

Jonathan Holden is University Distinguished Professor of English and Poet-in-Residence at Kansas State University. His collections of poems include *Leverage, The Names of the Rapids, Falling from Stardom, Against Paradise, American Gothic,* and, most recently, *The Sublime,* which won the 1995 Vassar Miller Prize. His critical books include *The Fate of American Poetry* and *The Rhetoric of the Contemporary Lyric.*

Dancing School

Marcia Thompane was light and compact,
her silk sides slick as fish's scales.
Doing the box step with me, she
stared into space, waiting
for somebody else.

Vernell Peterson was tense, rickety.
I had to crane up to speak
to her face. My fingers clung
to the rungs of her spine. Trying
to lead Vernell in the swing step
was like leading a dogwood tree.

Poor Liddy Morrison was always
the last to get picked. She was dense,
moist. An inner tube was tied
to her waist. Her gauze dresses
rasped like dry grass.
As I neared her, she'd stare
up with a dog's expectant look. I'd try
to be nice, to smile as though
I were glad it was her
I was stuck with; but Liddy
outdid me: she'd pretend
to be grateful.

El Paso

The ragged graph of spiring crags
is chopped,
and there you are
littered in the valley below a quarry,
your offices rubbing elbows,
Juarez, like refuse, beyond.

It's too bright.
The land is gripping you
in the gritty palm of its hand,
the sun on its fingers.

The road from the north was a guitar string,
a streak in a dust-parched
ocean of swimming mountains.
It brought us to nothing.
And the river said to flow here is no consolation.

The only river is up
in a sky the color of gin.
The only ocean is dust,
the wash of its waves a lisp
of breeze through the heads of the cottonwood trees
and the tremor of jets from Biggs.

Except for the night,
when your halcyon baubles come on,
when your valley arrays itself like the coals of a hearth
and your hotel lights are as lonely as blue stratosphere,
you have one horizon:

it is the slice, the saw-toothed snarl
and scorch of the F-104's.

Goat Slaughter

W'aa! bawled the kid as they hauled it
tottering on twiggy legs toward the stock.
W'aa! He felt like I did when my mother
drove me to Dr. Lucas to have my teeth out
with gas. W'aa! The kid balked. With
gas. The rope jerked it forward. With
gas. Its mother crowded against the fence.
The nurse smiled at me, attached the bib.

Stuck in the stock, the kid waa'd louder.
Dr. Lucas's office smelled like sweet rubber.
The kid tried to yank its head back through
the hole, its ears got caught. W'aa! Everything
grew vague. They'd forced this sweet, roaring
rubber cup over my face: "Now breathe
deeply. . ." W'aa! Its hooves flailed and crashed
as they put the .22 between its eyes. "Now
breathe deeply . . ." W'aa! "Good . . .
Excellent . . ." I tried to get away. W'aa!
"Good . . . Excellent . . ." Pow, it collapsed,
kicking, and I woke up in a strange room,
spitting blood into a pan.

Hitting against Mike Cutler

One down. I step into the narrow,
dust-floured shooting gallery, glance
out where the tall right-hander's squint
aims in to size things up. If it were up
to him, he'd take all afternoon he looks so
lazy—a gunslinger who just sauntered
into town, his jaw working over
a forgotten scrap of gum. He spits,
feels up the ball like a small, hard hornet;
and I hear the catcher settle in creaking
leather harness. He clucks contentedly,
does something dirty in his groin. Far
out there on the bright, bare, heat-rippling
hill the big guy nods. The hornet in his hand
begins to buzz. He bows. Slowly he
revolves away, then whirls, draws. I fire back.
The hornet hisses, vanishes with a BANG. STEE-RIKE!
The catcher grins. Good chuck, good chuck, he clucks.

Ice Hockey

Silver Lake has changed into a milky,
marble floor. Wind from around the bend
drives white dust up-ice with long broom-
strokes toward the dam. The lake
talks, mutters to itself as I take
my naked fingers out into air,
grab the laces, wind them round
my ankles, winch them so tight that my feet
wilt, then work back into my gloves.
I'm done: my fingertips are stones.
I lean, then, launch out over my stick
against the wall of the wind, make the whole
map of ice begin to move, the lightning-
splits of cracks begin to move
toward me, the sleek curves of other
skaters—etched with ice-spray where
their blades bit—begin to bend like moving
rails as the network of the city thins
to a few arcs across dark wilderness
where bubbles—the unblinking eyes
of fish—come flowing by. A loose
puck wobbles over the ripples.

I interrupt it, weave it with my wand,
let the wind into my lap to make me
stall, then with a willow flick
skim it back to the distant game,
follow it and join. The lake
begins to turn, a white wheel always
revolving, my legs robots, automatic,
kicking against the wheel
to make it spin until it streams so
fast my feet can't keep up, the wheel
flies out from under me, I sit down
hard on this slick seat that sears

my behind as it hisses to a halt,
then rise, chase down the game again,
thrust in my stick, grapple in the clatter.
The puck squirts free—in front of me—
alone, this rare coin, all mine.
I coddle it, nick the wheel, heave
at the wheel until it's whirling
under me in streaks, the goal swinging
into range, slap, miss, watch the puck
whiz, three guys stabbing after it
as I lean away into the force of ice
and level out, let the wind hit me
in the back and hurl me home again
across the fleeing map.

Cross Bracing

Anything that had studs or
that should stand straight
wobbled. Nails peeked out.
My tables trembled when I wrote.
My counters swayed. Heavily used,
they'd wallow until they'd worked
themselves back into the pieces
that I'd cut. I couldn't understand
why houses stood, until I learned
to cross brace, to notch 2 x 4's,
snap in the brace so that the slack
studs tensed together at attention.
Now, secretly, I sometimes lean
harder than I should against the things
I've built that stand, seize them
with a suddenness to make them
shake. They won't budge. They just
give me back this secret glee
of my own full weight. I would put
cross bracing into trees, in moving

clouds and water, into my whole
life if I knew how.

Remembering My Father

As I seize the ladder by its shoulder
blades and shake it back and forth
to test its roots, its cling, test
with gummed toes each rung up
from the shadow of the north wall
into the bright desert of the roof
the sun's weight spreads over my back,
and I see my father frowning in the sun,
his freckled back zigzagged with peeling
tan, his shoulders red, lowering a rock
into the stone swimming pool he built
by hand with boulders slithered
down on sledges from the woods,
split, rinsed off and fit—a pool
I could dive into until my ears
were so waterclogged they croaked.
I reach the top, fit
the window frame in place—the corners
mate—aim the first nail away
from the glass, sink it to its chin,
finger the next nail and prick
the wood; but as I heft the framing
hammer back to stroke, I see my father
in the cellar, frowning as he fits
his saw blade to a line, eases it back
and forth to start the cut, his breath
hissing through his nose as it always does
when he's intent. I hear my own breath
hissing through my nose. Something
silent in me starts chuckling in pure
gaiety because I'm frowning too, because
I know exactly what I look like.

A War Baby Looks Back

In the tender years of Eisenhower's first
term, I started mine
in Dr. Swain's office, my jaws pried wide,
my gums stuffed with cotton cigarettes,
staring sadly up into a soft, fluorescent
light while Dr. Swain peered down in
and frowned. I had to wear elastic bands
that caught in my mouth on steel hooks;
to wash my abhorrent, plastic bite-plate
off each night until my teeth were
straight. It was all worth it.
Thanks to Dr. Swain, one spring evening
toward the end of Eisenhower's second
term, on the cold leather of my parents'
car, a girl named Tina
let me feel her up.

Ed Ochester

Dancing on the Edges of Knives

1973

Ed Ochester is director of the Writing Program at the University of Pittsburgh and editor of the Pitt Poetry Series. He is the author of *Miracle Mile* and *Changing the Name to Ochester*. His most recent collection is *Allegheny*, a chapbook published by Adastra Press in 1995.

On a Friend Whose Work Has Come to Nothing

At school you dove off the bridge at night
in a swan, down to the half-dozen girls
treading water to keep up with you.
Then, cock of the walk, you'd strut off
with some chick while the rest of us
were left to drink lukewarm beer and cluck.

Those were the Dylan Thomas days when
wearing baggy tweeds you picked up west of Wales
you told *Under Milk Wood* so that all the dead below
were wet with tears. Then
you'd cut out with a casual girl
and leave us to dismantle the scene.

There were also the Norman Mailer days,
the quiet admonitions to suck the smoke in deep,
the blue morning jogs around the lake.
You were the last descendant of the
        Grand Duke Maximilian,
and every one of us was the true illegitimate
son of Hemingway, who
by the way,
was your very close friend.

You made yourself the prince of days
because you cracked imagination's cipher;
you taught us to ignore the telegrams
from the past that never came,
found at the heart of our onion
the nothing you'd been sure was there.
So. Our banquets and our pioneer characters
were spun from the brightness in the air.

Christ, while the rest of us thought each thud
of our typewriters was tough enough
        to puncture hearts,
you heard America snapping its gum
and laughed and fluted tunes
through their public forests
on the coast of pacific despair.

Thus, seeing a one-inch notice of your death
in a small-town Midwest paper,
it is difficult to say exactly what death
        has taken in,
except assuredly a politician among the apes,
a hummingbird above the snails.

But the rest of us—
Lord, vaguely amazed at your death,
corrupt as you but less successful,
still losing twenty dreams a year
        like irreplaceable feathers—
the rest of us at least two thousand miles
        behind you
are still crawling outward toward
        our mythical west coast.

King Kong

To be seriously maladjusted
is to despise organization.
You were a fool
to break your chains so easily
and to pull that grandstander
against the Army Air Force.
Grunting and loving women

are enough handicaps.
With planning you could have become
the general in charge of skyjacking
or a vice-presidential possibility.
Democratic hopefuls would have
begged for endorsements,
and housewives lusted
for your gigantic body.

The trick
when one sees their society for the first time
is to restrain the primal scream of horror,
to dream of islands,
but to go along.

The Knute Rockne Story

Shouldn't the *K* be pronounced?
If not, his parents could have called him
Pnute, Gnute, Fnute, or Babbaganute.
His mother was toying with Rock Knutne,
but they decided on Knute Rockne
with a silent *K*.
If the Gipper's parents had done this,
they could have named him the Kipper,
the Zipper, the Ripper, or the Dipper.
None of this happened,
according to the movie.
I can never remember who the Gipper
was. Ronald Reagan? Iron Horseman?
I can barely remember Rock Knutne.
I loved football, and this is what it has done for me:
Thousands of letters lost in the mail,
our country's history an incomplete forward pass.

Robert Bly Watched by Elves

On snowy evenings I like to
drive downtown to place my
cheek against the steel
of our Midwestern mailbox.

Tonight I receive illumination
from the street lamps
as I lie in snow
surrounded by elves

lifting their arms, *Salud!*
Their mittens are filled with snow.
The snow is shaped into balls.
Now the elves run from a ghostly

snowplow plowing through
snow toward us. It is good
to lie in snow, seeing things
invisible to impure men.

For You

How sad to be a casual girl
how sad to be bounced
in the rear of station wagons
along the shores of shrunken lakes.
How sad to listen to the men play
blackjack in the cabin and believe
Kafka's *Castle* is a hamburger joint
and Truffaut a kind of mushroom.
How sad never to understand anything at all.
How sad to walk along the lake at night
and not understand why the stars have all
been eaten by the god whose name you

forget at the moment but whom
Tibetans try to frighten with bells, cymbals,
and hideous dances on the edges of knives.
How sad to return to the cabin
and find the dead goose hung to bleed,
clamps in its nostrils, spinning
clockwise, counterclockwise—
that beautiful body hung like meat,
dribbling blood truly toward
the center of gravity.

I Wanted to Be a Ballerina

No matter that I was a plump child, chickenbreasted,
with pigeon toes and goose flesh, it was the whirling
hippo in *Fantasia* that fired me for Terpsichore.
"But you're a boy," they said, "and you have a swin-
ish case of psychosomatic gout to boot; give over
these hapless dreams." Friends, I speak to you tonight
as one who has conquered the quirks of circum-
stance and the incidents of birth. Laughter, pecker,
phlebitis of my left leg have been overcome by the
self-denial of toil; the thrifty sweat of industry has
manured my barren ground. Therefore I accept your
LL.D. with humility, but with pride. Thank you, Yale.
America, close your eyes and you will see me dancing.

Faulty Ductwork

I have had faulty ductwork for years.
When I vacation, neighbors wire
DUCTWORK FAILING
WATER EVERYWHERE.
There have been three attempts at arson.
Invisible rowdies
throw stones at my mother.

The bats have vacated my house.
I have a burning sensation
when I urinate, and I am no longer
allowed to vote.
My oldest boy shoots up nurses,
and deer have deserted the meadow.
The specialists give estimates endlessly,
but there is never enough money
for repair.

Among His Effects We Found a Photograph

My mother is beautiful as a flapper.
She is so in love
that she has been gazing
secretly at my father
for forty years.
He's in uniform,
with puttees and swagger stick,
a tiny cork mustache
bobbing above a shore line of teeth.
They are "poor but happy."
In his hand is a lost book
he had memorized,
with a thousand clear answers
to everything.

Gerald Costanzo

In the Aviary

1974

In addition to four limited-edition collections of
poems, Gerald Costanzo is the author of *The Laps of
the Bridesmaids* and *Nobody Lives on Arthur Godfrey
Boulevard.* He is poetry editor for Carnegie Mellon
University Press; for twenty years he edited *Three
Rivers Poetry Journal.*

Near Lacombe

Fastened to his rocker,
the old man rocked for hours
making stories from his life.
We heard his watch ticking
on its chain and smelled
the odor of his pipe
across the dusty room.

What we heard was
how hard it had been at first
coming west—
how he'd been the only one who helped
discover oil near Rimby,
making instant promise of the place—
how his good wife had loved these
lonely hours clean till her death.

And what we heard was
nothing
of what he thought he'd said.

For Four Newsmen Murdered
in Saigon
—May, 1968

The sickening hush. Your auto
caught in idle in the humid noon
with tires and windshield shot out
and surrounded by your riddled
bodies. These penalties for
point of view are accurate report

even in death. The street stinks
of terror and dust. In a moment

cowering refugees emerge from
hiding and quickly pass,
mumbling with stunned tongues
of watching you become the means

of your lost existence.
You might have been five dead—
but one, stumbling like a frightened
fawn at open fire, has feigned death
full account and lived
to tell us how it is trying to tell
us how it is.

In the Aviary

High above you some fool
in a biplane is seeding the
clouds. You curse him
aloud. You threaten him
with the flak of your fists.
Further along, three
archetypal owls out on a
limb begin hooting at you.
You pelt them with small
stones, consistently missing.
A parrot from the bushes
calls you a fly-by-night
something-or-other, and two
Snowy Egrets cough soot
on your shoes.
Deeper into the beautiful
garden, vultures circle your
heart like apostles of grief
marking time.

My Kindergarten Girl Friend

My kindergarten girl friend
had fat cheeks and chubby legs
but she was sweet. My thoughts
were of pulling up her dress;
not kissing in the coat closet
or grabbing her pony tail.

I imagine she's married now. I
see her husband harried at breakfast,
belching yolks of eggs she's slung
and swizzling his hot coffee.
She stands there in her tattered
robe, hair in pin clips, scowling.
He looks up and says

ya know, you used to didn't be
a bad lookin' woman.

At Irony's Picnic

Silence is sight-reading
Swahili. Sin lumbers by on

stilts. Where did he get
that Hawaiian shirt? those

rose-colored glasses? Down
by the lake Desire is fondling

Regret's mother. Jealousy
and Happiness dance the mazurka.

Justice, wearing the same
old swimsuit, is cutting the

ballyhoo. Irony himself
isn't even here.

The Bigamist

He lives to learn
the loopholes in his
speech,
the way the easy journey
from Memphis to Mobile
makes him forget
one-half of everything.
Darlings, as sure
as there are two of
you there are two of him
walking among us
somewhere, disguised
in his accustomed
civilian clothes.

An Author of Pantomime

What the black
tights and black

slippers tell you,
Sahib, is that

for the present I'm
top banana or anything

I wish to be. I waste
no breath. I ruffle

my hair a bit. Here
is my magic wand,

my *pince-nez*. I'm
skating along on

thin ice and then,
without apparent

effort, I put one foot
in the grave. I'm

masquerading as death,
Sahib, I'm speaking

to you in your native
tongue.

When Guy Lombardo Died

New Year's Eve went
with him. On December 31st

all of the people on the
earth's dark face

forgot how to dance.
Days later when they remembered

to Fox Trot, there was no
need. In the minute of midnight

gravity was suspended. The ball
atop the Times Square Building

refused to descend. For the
first time rain swirled

unimpeded by bodies to the
pavement of those streets, the

air a vacancy of kisses and
noise-makers. In the morning

people came from their houses
with no hangovers, and stone-sober

proceeded with the old business
of the world.

The Meeting

Somewhere along the road
you meet up with yourself.
Recognition is immediate.
If it happens at the proper
time and place, you propose
a toast:

May you remain as my shadow
        when I lie down.
May I live on as your ghost.

Then you pass, knowing you'll
never see yourself that way
again: the fires which burn
before you are your penance,
the ashes you leave behind are
your name.

Daniel J. Langton

Querencia

1975

Daniel J. Langton teaches and works in San Francisco. His books since receiving the Devins Award are *The Hogarth/Selkirk Letters*, *The Inheritance*, and the recently published *Life Forms*.

October Eighth

I noticed the leaves today, I have been sick
and losing touch, but there they surely were,
falling from crowded trees, playing at sur-
vival, trying to make my brain as thick
as their gatherings, their wrinkled ends, their May,
lying like truthful books the winners burn,
told in a language I will never learn.
My brother has been dead a year today.

I think of all the poems that use the Fall
to euphemize a death, but Jimmy died
this blazing time of year, and all the kinds
of metaphor won't reach the boy I call
and mourn and hunger for, the boy who tried
too well. They are just leaves. Life teaches, art reminds.

Warm Day

My dog harasses bees,
He tries to stop their life
In leaps at pumping wings,
He turns in flighty air
To find they are not there.
He paws and holds his ground,
Embarrassed by their sound.
Eve's anger spoils the fun—
God, how I hate those things!—
Grinning, I tell my wife
Something I know will please—
He will catch none. Or one.

Pantoum for Parker Mills

The world is just as new as once it was
Whenever love's strong waves send forth a son,
Whatever else the birth of children does
It leads grown men to feel there's something won.

Whenever love's strong waves send forth a son
The dawn of breathing life impresses all,
It leads grown men to feel there's something won,
It melts for just a while the graying wall.

The dawn of breathing life impresses all
Who in their grace can still be moved by grace,
It melts for just a while the graying wall:
We stand for one sweet moment face to face.

Who in their grace can still be moved by grace
Will know this feeling, and will know just when
We stand, for one sweet moment, face to face.
I am as sure as Job that all grown men

Will know this feeling, and will know just when
To praise the child, and thus to praise the truth,
I am as sure as Job that all grown men
Rejoice and glory in the birth of youth.

To praise the child, and thus to praise the truth.
Parker, I wrote this poem because of you.
Rejoice and glory in the birth of youth,
It gives grown men a fresh and lovely view.

Parker, I wrote this poem because of you.
Whatever else the birth of children does
It gives grown men a fresh and lovely view,
The world is just as new as once it was.

Long Distance

They called to me
To tell me my father
        was dying.
The wind was from the East
As I glanced at the trees.
Thanks, thanks very much, I said,
And that kind soft man, his arm raised,
Waved goodbye from the ship of his days.
Old hymns and a lost communion
Turned me as I turned away—
I stood again in that cold church,
My father beside me,
The clustered nuns before us,
The wind at my satin back—
My hand is still
So much smaller than his.

Popcorn

We have moved too much, traveled too much,
My head is a hive of old numbers,
JUniper seven something something seven something,
The stocking caught on the phone,
The desperate one by one of the lies.

GArfield something, 9023.
KLondike 5, whazzit whazzit ten.
Your phone spelled DANGERS,
Your phone spelled KLAAXXI,
Your phone spelled love once,
Something something once.

On Taking My Wife to Dachau

The gallows were really there, the long aisles
Really there, light Germans in huge beds
Arose at six, scratching their chests, their eyes
Unfocused, showered and came alive, killed
People reluctantly, a little sadly, thoroughly.
Missed you somehow, my life, my son's first armor.
O the roads are so good, like in California,
The parks are square. On the level ground
There is a memorial, an insistence.

Bit Players

It is that time of night
when it has been night for a long time,
bets are off, and the room has no corners.
The picture is flat and constantly interrupted,
like my memory and, like my memory,
it is in black and white.
A man smiles with first love
as he is being married
and I want to say to him,
I know what will happen to you,
you will live another thirty-one years,
the girl who holds your hand
has been mutilated,
the judge. . . .

                my aunt was twenty
when we saw this show,
I came to her hips, and she
hummed in tune with life.

Joe was still alive, and the
baby hadn't grown where it should not. . . .

It is late, late, late,
I stir in memory's light, real light,
everything near me saying, plain as day,
We know what will happen to you.

Bird Calls

I meant to come at dawn, birds being what they are.
But men being what they are it is nine o'clock
And I get birds like myself; loud, confident,
Charming, unarmed, jumping from flower to flower,
Light on their feet, always on the make, the sweet
Song just for song's sake, the chest firm,
The eyes soft, naked as jays, wearing no man's band.

The birds call, and I call, and the damned things hop
And I stand, watching the hop, my poorly ground axe
At my knees, swelling with bird calls, doomed
Where I stand, nothing to do but get older,
Hop slowed, belly round, dreams parallel parked,
Singing my late morning starving song
While the industrious birds sleep off their worm.

My My

It was the first good day in a long time—
Even bald men took their kids for a walk—
And I put on the Mamas and the Papas—
Stood at the window seeing marvels—
Dogs looked giggly
And the prick next door waved—
And I found I was saying out loud,
"I must have done something good,

I must have done something real good."
This is a poem for the angel
Who was given the privilege
Of naming the color of grass
And who jumped up and down
Waving his hand and shouting,
Green! Green! Green!
Oh! Green! Green.

Diana O'Hehir

Summoned

1976

Diana O'Hehir is the author of four books of poems and two novels and the coeditor of a poetry anthology. In addition to the Devins Award, she has received the Di Castagnola Award and a Guggenheim Fellowship and has been runner-up for the Pulitzer Prize. She lives in Bolinas, California.

Summoned

Summoned by the frantic powers
Of total recall, sleeping pills, love;
Come down, come down, come down;
Wear red if you can, wear red
For suffering, jade for rebirth
Diamonds in your front incisors,
A rope of orange stars—you were martyred, weren't
      you?
So wear a circle of gold thorns, prongs capped
In scarlet shell.

And bring with you, down, down, down,
A recollection of how you fell
Like Lucifer, morn to morn and night to night
For at least a year, your hair alight
Your rigid corpse a spoked wheel
Meteor trails ejecting from each thumb,
Sun eyes, a black light in your chest
Where the bare heart burned.

Oh love, my love, my failure,
I can hardly bear, barely recall
The nights I ate ghosts, the nights
My shuttered, shivered window held
Three million savage stars and you;
Your spread arms splitting my sky, the light
Reflected in my own eye: your light, your might, your
      burn.

Come down. My sky-chart shows
Your cold corpse turning slowly, a black sun
Giving no light at all, reflecting none,
Aimlessly gentle, a twig on a pond
Circling. Gone, they say, gone, truly gone.
The eyes as blank as buttons, the mouth

Only an O. Never mind. Come down,
I can revive you. My passion is Judah, all artifice, all
    God.
I care with my breasts. I care with my belly's blood.
Come down.

A Poem for Sarah's Mother

"My mother was a widow. She cleaned offices.
She sent all four of us to college."—Student theme

Those evenings the offices are cold; the chill gets in
    under your ears,
Sends an iron bar from here to here; I imagine her
Like a kind of saint hassling a dragon, a prophetess,
Toes locked against an angel on the edge of a cliff,
The angel says, prove; it says, behave.
It says, one night on a cliff is fine; afterwards
They go away, they turn your hopes inside out.
No one will remember a thing about you and your mop.

One of those fighters had to go over; one
Had to stand on its forehead in the chasm, bat hair
    flying.
Fall like my wishes, the mother said.
Your arms wrenched back into broken wings,
Angel. I'll wallop it out of you.

The mother is tall, her hair tied behind her ears in a
    kerchief.
The worst part of her day is midnight:
The tiredness of soup, sullen radio,
Sleeping children, the angel who follows after, wings
    akimbo,
Edges of feather dipped in paint. It has a neon line
    around it.
            It says,

I'll wrestle with you, lady.
My student thinks herself an ordinary woman
Except for that battle. That's one of those childhood
      flashes
That startles sleep, that lights up Oakland afterward.
She says: They fought. The angel glowed like an electric
      heating element.
They fought for fifteen years.
My mother won.

Imminent Earthquake

The sky is as dry as baking powder.
A scuffed shoe may send the whole thing up.

Houses, sidewalks, stucco railings string out in a
      sound-line,
A breakable presence, garage-door magic beam.
It waits for its flag
And the rumbling mess shoves, gawky fingered, home.

Like everything you wait for.
It sits behind you holding its breath in static.
It moves in the circle of your mother's death.

Last year's earthquake: we were at the opera.
We flattened ourselves into our velvet chairs,
Clutching the arms, weighed down by that pushing
      apron;
A conveyor-belt roar lurched off next to my ear.
It spoke in metal of a metal world, metal people, and
      flowers
Clashing themselves to a brassy finish,
And death as the voice of an open gong.

Down in the works of the opera house,
Shifting weights shoved each other like cousins,

A raucous playground scraped by noise.
Afterward, the air wasn't dry. We laughed, a captive
      people.
We laughed as if the sea had split for us.

Lunar Eclipse

Whoever said yellow or said round?
Here I am fishing for the moon on my front doorstep,
Wanting to memorize it; a moon like a pulse beating at
      the end of a tunnel,
Moon like the gills of a white carp.

Our porch stairs are still warm. Laughter shreds over the
      eclipse;
The binocular in my hand is a machine
Winding us up to that open nostril
Pulling at you and me and him and her.

The sky's alive; it licks us up like milk.

We hold ourselves separate, arms slicked into seaweed;
Each of us is a pool for the other's watching.

It isn't really red, you say; that bump is the Mare
      Crisium.
A wedge of loneliness catches my rib. The night
Pulls a rope around my chest.

The moon beats above us,
Fleshed with veins.

Night Train

Noise loops itself
Catlike, self-centered, around the walls of her bedroom,

Abrading the paper, foraging into her sleep
For nuggets of love, of wishing.
It chews them like bubble gum; it has iron teeth.
It has a shout that sends metal down into a woman's
        thighs;
It swaggers, matching its rhythm to the pulse in her
        neck.

It says, night after night your escape goes down,
You seek the wall to hold its shout.
It says: night's child.

The woman turns in the dark, touching dry linen.
There's a cricket beside the bed; she sees her husband's
        shadow.
The walls of the bedroom are
A cricket's cage.
Train light measures the sky; cinders are fiery needles,
        fiery dreams.

Day comes in hot as a prairie. The trees grow scented
        day candles.
Silence covers the sky in blue smoke.
Everything signals that night won't come again

Except night's child. Night's favorite child
Goes down to the crossing, waves chums at the engineer.
She's seeking, still seeking in secret the coal-eyed
        stranger
Who drives his bright hot squawking engine through her
        dreams.

Hands

Somewhere in Asia, a wall
Patterned with the handprints of women,
Saint's, martyr's hands

Cased in crystal, the blood stopped up with a ruby.
My hands ache for a skill not yet invented.

It comes at me in dreams; it's all-encompassing,
A talent that will take the scars off foreheads, grow palm
    trees
On the salt steppes of Utah,
Hack out emblems with the powers of children;
They'll leave home, abandoning their ancestors,
Appearing in different cities with their own ways of
    dying.

Arbitrary as pain, that urge to make
Is edgy about time,
Imagines a monument out of wedding-cake lace,
Sloshes a picture of you across the reflecting pool, gives
    you
A white intense smile like a Mexican shoeshine boy's.
It draws a recognizable picture of love.

My hands remain as ordinary as mud.
They wear too many rings.
The electricity slides over them like glycerine,

When what I want is to hold the pencil
That draws a perfect circle,
A child inside it, an old man sleeping.

Escaping

She rips the dressing off, climbs out of the hospital
    window on a rope,
And onto an old black bicycle,
Shouting at the birds that rise up to scrape the air with
    patchwork wings,
Rides twice around the square, pedaling hard;
The bandage on her forehead glows like a new red hat.

That country is hotter than ours, along the canal
The corners of every view are red,
The sky smells of apricots,
She's letting her knees get burnt with it,
Blood tracks a question mark across her cheek.

Under the cliff, miles of still blue water, tight as a
        Chinese drum,
Bridges of fern heavy with plant milk, platters
Of thick white plaster flowers.

That world is shallower than ours. Behind her
The city rides on the ridge like an airborne freighter.

She'll pedal until the road winds down to a yellow track
And speckles of blood make mesh on the handlebars:
Then, down into the broad grass;

It's as hot and flat as paper
It tastes of summer.

The Old Woman Who Made Boxes

On the edge of the cliff the wind blows a typhoon;
Sand and stickers wedge in her socks, her hair blows out
        straight,
Stiff as a board with salt; she's clutching her tray of

        boxes.
Red cinnabar boxes, black jade,
Soapstone carved with birds' eyes,
A box is a cage around space.
Mad old lady in gym shoes, her days are a royal mess,
But the boxes are as elegant as the Book of Kells.

A whistle scrapes the air like jet trail;
The sea-cliff house is settling; one corner nudges the air;

Waves, bird-screams, electrical displays; it's
Land's edge for humans.

The old woman wears a brown burlap dress; the storm
Tucks it tight at her bony knees, into her V;
Wave froth frosts her shins like the storm-kings' beard.
She thinks: soapstone bird eyes, red jade with a grape at
the center;

I've made a hedge of Byzantine ovals;
They'll cut the wind.

Breathing

I've been struck by lightning only once.
It soaks you down, dissolves the bones to soup,
Rattles your eyes like castanets.

The hands of lightning wrap you in plastic sheets,
You're the child inside, pulling.
Don't breathe, little one. Lie still.
Love, what comes out of lightning? Power,
A passion to breathe, even when breathing's death.

It happened only once. Life now is different.
Roads are straight as curtain rods; it's easy
To get up in the morning; the gardener squeaks his rake
along the walk;
The mail is tied in bundles. I can help you.

Sometimes I meet someone in the supermarket; in her
eye
The back gone out of the pupil, specks of mica, blackness
Where light has wedged a window into spiky country.

We watch each other, sharing a past:
Lightning. The taste of lightning.

C. G. Hanzlicek

Stars

1977

C. G. Hanzlicek is Professor of English and Director of Creative Writing at California State University, Fresno. He is the author of seven collections of poetry, the most recent of which is *Against Dreaming,* which was published by the University of Missouri Press.

Stars

It's been estimated that atoms
in your body have been through
several stars—that they were
ejected many times as gas from
exploding stars.
                    —*Jeremiah P . Ostriker*

Seattle
Chief of the Suquamish and Duwamish
Said when a white man dies
He no longer loves the earth
He wanders among the stars
Shedding his life
Skin by skin
Until there's nothing but a shiver
Of light

But when a red man leaves the earth
He never forgets rivers
White with a new year
Deer dancing through scrub oaks
The hawk
Shaking the sky with its shriek
And the man often drifts down
To breathe the air of the living
To touch stone
Touch water

Crouched at the firepit
Of an abandoned camp in the hills
With my thumb I polished
The obsidian knife I'd found
Something moved through the pines
Almost like wind

It touched my hair
Then ran downhill to drink at the stream
If it wasn't the spirit of a man
It was at least a spirit of silence
We have lost

I want to move
Quietly on this earth
Touching stones
The trunks of trees
The moons on ponds at night
Touching hair and touching flesh
Almost like wind
And when I die
I won't be ready for stars
They'll have to bury me

Bend or Break

1.

When I took the powder
Of the moon
Into my insulated hands
And held it up
I found nothing to believe in

Drifting back to earth
Like a spore shot from its cannon
I dream of a jackrabbit
Dead beside a river
Dream of drifting through his ribs
And taking root

2.

A clock in the reed bed ticking
The muskrat diving
Under his V trail for weeds
Leaves baring
Their spines in the shallows
And against the night sky
Whirling clusters
Of fireflies

A whole future
Along the green turn in a river
Where willow limbs
Bend or break above the water

At a Lake in Minnesota

Walking the shore toward me
Is the farmer from across the road
A man with seven teeth
And forty acres gone to weeds
The bib of his overalls supports
A belly bloated
By pilsner and boiled potatoes

Each fifty paces or so
He baits and sets a steel trap
Tells me he's after muskrats
Says these days their pelts ain't worth
A nickel in a whorehouse
But the varmints ruin
The shoreline with their nests

This is a man who *owns* things
His body his mind
A lake and every foot of its shore

And if a woodpecker
Breaks through his sleep at dawn
A little jolt of birdshot
Will wipe it away
Clean as a fog of breath
Leaving his shaving mirror

After he's rounded the point
I get the broom from the cabin
Beginning where he began
I touch the broomstick
To the baited tongue in each trap
A loud clack moves over the water
A satisfying sound
A life saved
A whole shoreline gone to hell

Mirage

The scrape of my feet is an alarm
The lake tips its mirror
Pours its silver into a canyon

A light wind shimmers the sky
Like a sheet of foil

A man who can drink light
Drink silver
Can stomach anything
I confess now my love of water

The cactus army
Throws up its arms in surrender
Waves a flag of vultures

Without knocking a pack rat
Walks through the door
Of a snake

Without knocking
I walk all day through myself
Yesterday I was here
About tomorrow I've said too much

Nautilus

The sea has written a story on the shell
In lines of brown ink

The characters turn inward
And then vanish in a darkened chamber

Hold it to your ear
And you hear only one long breath

To know how the tale ends
You'd have to smash the shell on a rock

It must be read like the story of a man
With no desire for an ending

Calibrations

His shoes slick and soft with oil
Caked by curled steel shavings
Were docked like boats for a week
On newspapers by the door
When a disc
Lost its place in his spine

Eyes bright with animal pain
He crawled
On hands and knees through the house
Cried when he had to rise

Into the shape of a man
To take a piss

With a little fear still in his eyes
He went back to the factory
To feed steel stock
Into his milling machine
To live by close tolerances
Exact measurements

Nights in his basement workshop
When he pulled a beaded chain
The bare bulb swung
Our shadows from wall to wall
I sat on a box
And watched him get lost
In the softness of wood

Often I'd ask to see his calipers
Their leather case
Was slick with his own oil
The numerals and lines
Had all worn smooth
Under the ball of his thumb
But for him the calibrations were clear
In his memory
In the sureness of his touch

The Old Man Made It

The old man made it
Past the guards again.
He runs down the street,

Tailed by yapping dogs,
His gown billowing
To bare his skinny

C. G. Hanzlicek

Ass, banging the bottom
Of a cast-iron
Skillet with a spoon.

I remember when
He was sane. He rocked
On the porch all day,

Shooing the sparrows
That shit with care on
His waxed Oldsmobile.

When they came back he'd
Toss them bread, and nod,
And sing himself to sleep.

Then last June he sang
To his pigeon-
Breasted neighbor girl,

And the town put him
Away. Somehow it's
Always me who has

To stop him, chase the
Dogs away, and say,
It's all right, Howard,

Everything's all right.
Arm in arm we jog
Our way to the home.

The cook gets back her
Skillet and her spoon,
I get my thankyou

From the guards, the old
Man gets his red pill.
How strange it's always

Me who stops him, when
I have in my closet
My own sort of bell,

And in my mind, these
Days, a similar
Sense of alarm.

Janet Beeler (Janet N. Shaw)

Dowry

1978

Since the publication of *Dowry*, Janet Beeler Shaw
has published seven novels (six for young readers),
a collection of stories, and poems and stories in
literary journals, most recently in *Shenandoah* and
Tar River Poetry under the name Janet Beeler Shaw
or Janet Shaw. She lives in Asheville, North Caro-
lina.

Dowry

The pelt of old snow still stays
on the field,
a tattered sheepskin,
but there's a thin stain of sun.

Time to take out
these lengths of cloth
I wove in the dark seasons,
time to bring kettles to the barnlot
and boil my dyes—
yellowweed,
red from madder root,
woodwaxen as green as winter wheat,
the orange of bittersweet.

I'll stretch these new colors
up to dry on the frames you've made,
a bride making her first bed.
Barefoot, we'll strip off our winter clothes
and wash each other free
in this bright thaw.
Then wrap up in our dazzling sheets.

Your name like chrism on my lips,
let clear light rise in me.

Passage

He turned his head
meaning to ask the time, or call
for the pan on his bed,
or beg for more Demoral (yes,
certainly for dope, he had been
coughing up

shreds of his lungs into paper cups
for six months by then).
He said nothing, instead;
she had already dissolved into darkness.

He still heard the tractor, the cat
purring under the bed.
Ted! she cried, and he heard that
last, wondering who is Ted?

Missouri Bottomland

I'll be the girl in her daddy's shirt
and her brother's Levi's,
riding in your pickup truck
with the six-pack between my knees,
waiting for the summer day to shut down.

You be the boy in wash pants and white bucks,
smelling of soap and Coke,
driving with one hand.

I've got the army blanket, honey,
you've got the church key,
and after dark the riverbank is blind.

I'll be the girl in the weeds and honeysuckle,
with cool hands and red lollipops,
and a slick, flat belly.

You be the boy who rolls me off the blanket.

I'll be the girl with sand on her bare ass
who makes the stars disappear
with her mouth.

The Lovers

Did you signal to me
as we were drowning?
Your hands said something,
was it my name?
I'd forgotten my name.

Locked into me
in the long dive down
through dark water,
past schools of swimmers
struggling back toward light,
clouds of fish diffusing,
night tides, dulse adrift,
bodies sewn into shrouds.

Primal blackness at the ocean bed,
blind bones,
shells like melon rind,
drifts of sand under my head.

So this is where we began,
so this is where one will begin,
where water is a hopeless weight.

Twins

The two of us in one belly.
Passion, that fat mother
floating us, feeding us,
absorbing blows.

We twisted in our small space,
drinking the same salty fluid,
fed with the same blood, blind.
Light and dark like our limbs twining.
All those fingers, ours—

four hands for the two of us.
The one membrane for both.
The way out like a way in,
blank and fiery, skulls crushing,
air lacerating our lungs,
faces as in weeping.
And the surgical necessities, after.

Late at night when my skin aches
where your skin was sliced away,
when my bones hurt
where your bones were broken away,

I want back in.

Christine de Pisan

I dreamed the shape of the universe,
bivalved as an oyster
shutting itself softly
onto its precise shadowless edge,
like lips closing in death.

It is like my cupped hands
which I close over that empty space
in which I exist,
over darkness.
No other hand fits mine in this way.
The rims of Heaven and Hell meet
and rest without warp.

I can hold the one half in my circling arm
as I hold my child,
and embrace the other half
as I hold my lover.
Oval.
But where my hands join
they are burned and red with this truth.

Archeologist

The cellar crouches on its haunches.
Its stone spine cuts a channel in clay,
but goldenrod has broken the bricks,
saplings have pierced tiles,
wild grass holds the space at bay.

I'm here to see my trench,
this kiva shaped to an ancient order,
cloistered and severe,
how passages, root rooms, coal chutes
still stink with a dark sap
that sticks like pitch or blood,
smells like bitter, homemade beer.

I've come back to camp in the tiger pit,
to live without rooms or roof.
I can sleep between the sky and the stone
and dig until I find that charred word
rare as a bronze bead: No.
It was the one thing of my own.

Georgia O'Keeffe

A woman with almost the body of a man
lives in her adobe facing West.

Only what she needs is with her,
her bowl and blue pot,
her bench, roped bed,
her white calf's skull.

Mornings, she weeds squash and beans.
After the blank noon heat
she paints the shapes ironed
onto her mind's hot horizon.

When the desert night comes on suddenly,
that silent metaphor,
she leaves her lamp unlit
and lies down on the earth,
letting the sand press her upwards,
knowing her own unfurling
against the unfurling dark.

Muse

He dove into her as into the sea,
feeling her give under him
as he sand into her broken shadow.
He called her Lady of the Gleam of the sea.

He felt her as element around him,
without horizon,
bearing him up, drawing him on as a tide.

He said, the gleam of the moon's eyelids
of the lady of the golden necklace
will bring harm both to me and to her.

But he floated.

She grew vaster in each adulation,
she drowned whole islands,
she rose and fell with the moon,
but still he would not stop.

She closed the hawk-moon of her eyes
and dreamed of making bread,
of folding linen,
but he sang on,
drifting always out from her shore.

G. E. Murray

Repairs

1979

G. E. Murray has published five other collections of poetry, *Oils of Evening*, *Walking the Blind Dog*, *Gasoline Dreams*, *Holding Fast*, and *A Mile Called Timothy*. He has served as poetry critic for the *Chicago Sun-Times* and *Chicago* magazine. Mr. Murray works as a communications consultant in the United States and extensively in Europe.

Holding Fast

To hell with flowers
and sentimental train rides.

I prefer to travel alone
by knee, like a gardener,
thankful for weeds.

Reducing the Herd

Beyond the customary methods—
a pistol to the head,
arsenic in drinking troughs,
throats slit like melons—

there are questions of the pit,
its capacity and width,
who turns the soft earth open

against the low of half-knowing calves?

I prefer thinning the herd
by breed, age, nature of disease.
Young Jerseys

first, the prod-proof ones,
given to bewilderment
and double scoops of feed.

Certain Holsteins next,
the strays, the weaklings,
laying low
in patchwork fields.

Then those Herefords,
crossbred into dreaminess . . .

All losers at market,
all dumped from hoppers,
their necks ripe with fear,
their confusion high as the sun.

              *   *   *

Call it slaughter,
call it necessity.

We're sore from the trouble.

Tired of shooting
daylong until dark,

I watch those chosen
drop hard into carcass.

None of us likes it much.
To right the selection,
bury the kill

before our children
spot a favorite
twitching in the trench—

that's the trick!

              *   *   *

We rock down the day's sun
in armchairs of privilege.

In the loins of what we keep
new strains of nuisance
root like weeds.

We accept this,
and clean our guns regular.

I sit content with evening's rest
under a warm lampshade,
headlines unread in my lap,
twilight turning down the fields
like a great feather bed

as our children lope off
after supper.

In a hardwood barn
the good beef grazes
on dark obedience,
sensing us.

Camped in old ways,
our hands washed
daily in milk,

we lie back to snore
and remember nothing.

American Cheese

She was made from scratch in Wisconsin,
Slowly at first, given to disguises
As a child, a figure swept
By sunshine toward the free fall
Terror in her heart. A declension of circles,
She grew round and firm and ready,
A processed miracle,
Sealed in wax of nervous gestures,
Exported to Chicago as a necessary foodstuff—
Old prairie fiction.
When she turned the wind's
Hard corner, aging decades in days,
She announced, during a daylight attack
Of logic, straight up and down
Like an exclamation point, she was her own

Worst obsession, the failed product
Of a putty knife. Years later,
Crazy on Clark Street, her one stocking
Rolled below the snow line
Of an ankle swollen with city winters,
She becomes available
As litter, blown around the trainless
Midnight of Union Station, talking
A blue streak to the terminal darkness.
In the midlands, there is no telling
The stories of the dead.

The Hungarian Night

From trees fall shavings of her darkest enthusiasms.
Her face that rivets breezes, the chilling soil
Of our riverside walk, go warm to furnished anterooms

Of dear Budapest. We share a borrowed Cuban cigar,
Railway stories, a coin to rent two hours of heat.
Look at her green stockings hung almost unremembered,

Slipping from chairback to floor, like eels.
Night turns wet, and pronouncements of tea leaves
Govern her officious dealings with the planet.

Night is a worm in the heart, she says, an ancient worm
Eating granite. Soot drops from nowhere, the sky.
There's a battle scene we recognize carved on the
        bedboard.

Above attics in the musty capital, smokestacks huddle
Like brown monkeys. Someone dies crying in this place.
Someone opens to blood storm and heresy. Sirens

Mired in alleys say it's so. Downstairs a café stinks
Of cabbage and pepper soup, stays lit by lavender neon.
We can believe the faded meanings of tapestry

And that moment of pilgrimage now, the skull bone
Buzzing empty, without ambition or reluctance.
Next door a man wheezes and sputters, healing from
Dreams of absinthe, white suits, and slow ceiling fans.

Chicago as the Time of Night
—to Michael Healy, in Cambridge, Mass.

With Chicago underfoot and spoiling
like a month-old egg, a hair of music
in the city's unkempt dish of butter,
I add this place to my necklace of schemes.
Pure East, pure cream, I'm wrinkled like skin
on a mattress, next to false teeth and rouge . . .
This is just scuttlebutt: on central time,
dying is an irrelevant surprise.
The infinite gray and meager shock of wedding
the midlands hits colder than a left hook.
I'm keeping track of the lost fantastic jazz
and mobs, wearing a castaway fedora . . .
I'm up-country in the good straw to stay.
For now, it's almost atomic, baby.

In Memory of a Coastal November

The wind keelhauling
November again. The facile women
Gathering tweed

Goods on the veranda, watching sloops
Drop out of season.
Block Island,
Kennebunkport, South Bay,

Wherever a solitary tourist slouches
Away unnoticed, faintly waving

Farewell to a sea town's
Bait of water,
Its weathered clapboard.

By afternoon, the usual musics
Play to both sides
Of louvered doors—
Edith Piaf
On Victrola;
Birds sweetening
Rain shortened days.

And there are collars turned against
Gooseflesh, against the idle gazing
In the parlor of a maiden aunt.

All these passages clearing at once
Are called November
As it fades, as a herringbone sky
Settles everywhere,
Over shoreline and pierview,
The shuttered marketplace,
A tear vase.

And the women continue darning
The men into tweed.
And the clapboard, the lapping water,

Still await the advent of small occasion.

Catfishing in Natchez Trace

Some fair luck where the fickle rush of backwash
jewels. It's a sapphire day, sonnet weather,
all bordering shore and illusion. Wise fish
are guessing right at my worst hunches,
unfooled by my sinkers or choice of lure,

waving like secret flags along this river bottom
before spooling away. Again, the sporting life
unfolds expectedly: a squatting in water's sungleam,
the zigzag drift of reed beds, dead palm leaves
slapping hull, that endless roll of floorboard
between coffee breaks and quivering bait,
the circuiting spill of fuel
running engine mount to bow. Behind
rows of oleander, the sky begins rehearsing
a passing storm. Brackish water silks like whiskey.
Trolling, I switch from green-eyed flies
to doughballs and leeches, plunk this ditch of a river
with plastic bugs, until I acquire a string
of two catfish and contempt for silence . . .

It's October's music I want swarming,
the year in sudden menopause, wheeling
crosswater, over snags and wakes of browned blossoms,
down past cold stone ruins of Civil War hovels,
where families once gathered like schools
of hungry trout, mouthing nightly bible lessons
by candlelight, a ghostly reader marking his place
with a braid of fresh horsehair . . .

Listen, the boat that brought me this far knows
how the slime of fish gut greases tackle,
scaling knife, how it inhabits fiberglass and flesh.
Here, in skunk water, somewhere below channel
and open stream, miles from any legal limit,
I angle through flotsam, soft plugs of larvae,
hitting moderate chop, port tack.
Then I veer left instead of northerly
and jam fast into a mistake of a sandbar.
The propeller surges and cranks, gargles white,
whines a newborn's whine. Nothing gives. Nothing
moves, except the sun turning out in its airy socket.
Overhead, wild geese cruise this flyway,
lost for home. Coffee's gone. My compass wanders,

as if reading disheveled margins of mind.
Light bleeds light illegible in a distance
of Confederate grays. Wedged so tight, I think maybe
to dump it, swim off, abandon that bouillabaisse
of solitude, these hours nowhere,
the piddling whiskered fish I prize like manhood.
Still, pasted against a tomato sunset,
it's a manageable reality, this:
hunkered down in twilight, shanghaied
by a rocky lot of creek, snarling at the day
that closes like a chilled pore, my shadow
now darting in a reel of backroad Mississippi;
and me, telling stories of men
to relieved, understanding bullheads.

Frank Manley

Resultances

1980

Frank Manley is the Director of the Creative Writing Program at Emory University. Since receiving the Devins Award, he has published a volume of short stories, a volume of conversations about his poetry, and a number of plays.

Lightning Bugs

We used to take an old lamp with the bulb out
And a steel wire from a milk-bottle top
Twisted and stuck in the lamp to make contact
And run it out to the hog-wire fence
When they were rising like static around us
And electrocute the lightning bugs in a shower of sparks.
Great power flowed in the current of our hands
As we probed with the electric tip of our minds
For whatever it was in the core of light
That burned all day in the heart of things
And rose in the night, in the dazzling darkness,
And swarmed from the shadowy forms of the earth
Like pulses of thought—the white, elliptical ghosts
Of trees, the fiery tip in each blade
Of grass, and the pastures rising above themselves,
All in their own true forms at last,
Like the souls of the just. And we were plugged into
It all we believed and flowed with a power that leaped
In invisible arcs from the static swirling of stars
In space and the flames of unknown galaxies, down
To our illumined heads and out the sockets
Of our eyes along the wire to the fiery fence,
Where the bugs we impaled turned crisp and died,
Oozing their liquid jelly of light
While we turned green as fox fire, our hands
And mysterious fingers, even the hair and grain of our
    skin
Streaked and smeared with gleams of solid light.
And then, then we stalked through the dark of our
    childhood
Like *ignes fatui* following the luminous forms
Of ourselves, grim as ghosts haunting our bodies
Back to the blinding effulgence of home.

Falling

The calls I dread come every night
As soon as I've fallen inside myself

Before I hit bottom and die
In my sleep. My father's weary voice
Comes through the burning core in the heart

Of the wire. He calls me to tell of his falling:
A toy on a string in my hand.

His voice is almost too high to be heard.
It hums on the wire inside my head,
The sound of my blood, the same thing

Over and over, like a busy signal:
First death, first death.

Going Out

Outside the house
year after year
the rot inside each drop of rain
inside the friction of the wind
the smell of a cellar
the color of lichens on stone
the light coming through
from inside the boards
like light in a wasp nest
and the house going back
inside the storm
inside the tearing
the grinding of tin

Inside the house
something had happened

something got loose and stayed inside
in the hole of the chimney
something was there
the walls ripped and hanging in sheets
the pile of dirty clothes in the corner
something had torn it with knives
and was there
in the shattered glass on the floor
sharp as hate

And on the wall
a sign
like a suicide note
saying

WE GOING OUT
AND ETERNATY
TO MEET GOD

RU READY
GODS CLOCK IS TICKING
AWAY ITS TIME

saying o yes
we all going out
after the murder
after the last knife of the looting
the rape of the old clothes of our body
we going out
for god's clock is ticking
inside the rain
scratching the wasp nest wall of our skull
god's clock is ticking
inside the wind of our lives
inside the wind of our breath
god's clock is ticking
inside the storms
that sweep around us at night

with the screeching of tin
that rips at the top of our skull
god's clock is ticking
inside the shine of our bones
burning inside us
and we going out
o yes we going out
we all going out of that house

Origin of the Species

Dogs are all doomed.
They cannot survive.
They screw your guests
Below the knees
And hump the furniture.
They shit in the streets
And piss on small children.
Sometimes they eat them.
They also eat garbage.
Dogs have bad breath.
Their eyes are sad.
They sleep in the sun
And need to be consoled.

Dogs are like dinosaurs.
The last ones are shrinking.
They never go out.
They sit in your lap
And smell good.
They have no fleas,
Nothing to bark at.
They turn into cats.

And the cats will survive.
They shit in boxes
And cover it up.
They are always alone.

Cats are like grease.
They make no noise.
They care about nothing.
Cats stay in houses
And never get lost.
They look out of windows.
They are always thinking.
Cats are like people.
Cats will inherit the earth.

Ghost Story

They asked for it, safe in their flannel cocoons
For the night, prepared to sleep and dream
Into their chrysalis of day.

So I told them of Tickanately Church,
That sits high on the flashing river,
Washed with the blood of its burying ground,
And how its lonely bell would ring
That very night, when long nails
Scratched at the pine of the coffin
Till clod by clod the grave unburied itself
And the shapeless thing took shape again,
Rising to scatter the plastic flowers
And all the names turned into stone at Tickanately
        Church,
Slashing the ground with its long nails
In the immortal, mysterious hate of the dead.

And suddenly I scared myself.
I saw myself in the lonely clay of Tickanately Church,
Tearing the flowers my children brought
On sunlit days in the upper air,
While close in the night,
In the house made tight with the strength of my arms,
My children slept into age.

Poor Tom

I can understand the monkeys, Thomas,
And a weasel or two, some parrots in cages,
Maybe even a Barbary ape, a gift
From the Spanish ambassador for services rendered.
Good for the children. Part of the plan.
Not that Erasmus would ever approve.
St. Jerome's lion was more his style:
In a desert, where the sun bears down
As sharp as his mind without shadow.
Your beasts, Thomas, were caged in a garden.
Shaded by shrubs, behind the house.
Henry Patenson fed them, a natural,
Grinning and smacking his lips as they ate.
Dame Alice could hardly tell you apart.
And sometimes on Fridays—I understand, Thomas—
Leaving the shape of your life at the altar,
The heretics bound and lashed in your study,
You'd visit in private the king and his council,
The great lords at Lambeth, in cages,
God's creatures all—antic, amusing:
Weasel or monkey or parrot or ape.
You could hardly tell them apart,
You, the only free man among them.
I understand that. Hall said you joked
Your way to the scaffold: a matter of style.

But Cliff, Thomas—Cliff. What cage
Or cell did you keep him in
After you took him by the hand
And led him away from knocking the heads
Off statues of saints on the bridge to the Tower?
Where did he stay in the garden?
And what did you see in him, Thomas?

Compassion, perhaps, a work of mercy?
Or did you see yourself there at last?

The mad eyes innocent and full of anger,
Caged in himself: your own *memento mori,*
The head and the sharpened ax the same:
The outcast, the shape of your life at the altar?
Cliff waits in the cage, Thomas.
He cannot rest. He cannot be kept,
Cannot be loosed till the king claims
The garden and the cages all open.
Then Cliff roams free,
And your head returns to its place on the bridge.
Your distant eyes look down from the pike.
They do not see Cliff pass in the crowd.
He walks on the water, over the Thames,
Other things on his mind now,
Not heads, looking for something
To find in a storm, somewhere to rest,
Some hovel. Poor Tom,
Poor Turleygod, poor Tom.

Plato's Cave:
Chicken Little and the Holy Ghost

Inside the dark tunnel
where someone before me
grew chickens like crops
in the light of eternal day
I brood on the grainy ladders
of sun where the roof has collapsed into glory
and wait for the sky to fall.
My feet in the dung of the ages
I hear the whir of the ghostly
wings the fiery cackle
of tongues in the dark
and hatch myself into silence.

Mary Kinzie

The Threshold of the Year

1982

Mary Kinzie studied languages and thought at
Johns Hopkins and the Free University of Berlin, but
did not start to save the poems she wrote until she
began teaching poetry two decades ago. Her fifth
volume, *Ghost Ship*, was published in 1996 by
Knopf. She is Professor of English at Northwestern
University.

Minor Landscape

Out in the north beyond that stand of trees,
new-green, with pink and chilly russet strata
much like light glowing in the cruces,
is the hiding place. Brindled cows
investigate a white-hot stack of ancient
mulch: they're peaceable, however large
their jaws upon their tiny frames. Virginals,
mild French, and laxer agricultural
recourses raise their necessary sounds,
which are hardly to be heard from far and here.

Landed gentlemen direct their stubby
shanks and modicum of lace toward
a tufted hill where, against the mossy
fall of air into a lightless valley,
their torsos seem unearthly thin and long,
their shoulders, simple blades. White clay pipes
glimmer in long arcs beside their hands
while words come batted by the past at intervals,
disjoint and plump. The queer adornments
of their tongue, its queerer strengths, are manly

stasis in the moral views, the craft
of state, the way to seed adjacent fields
obliquely as to rows, how force the plum,
how breed the spicy hound, how stave the cooling
marriage with more home delights. Their moods?—
a mystery, inconsequent, perverse.
But pain is real enough and difficult
dark passions that meet them in the curling wood
beyond the fading hill, the sun-smoked mulch,
the quiet brindled cows, and playing wives.

The Tattooer
—after the story by Tanizaki

Her toenail and the pearly heel
dissolved by the dark grin of the retreating
palanquin were all he'd seen,
sufficient for his whole career,

Imagination's view of her
complete: the sense of endless thigh
milky as the ponies of the Emperor
above their slender slicing hooves,

his expectation of her skin
a wilderness of intercostal
ice on which her sanguine soul
could be engraved in Ryukyu cinnabar.

Years later—since our fate in these accounts
is after all the fruit of our desires
and sentences in which we crave are those
by which we're doomed—he found her at his door.

Master of a beauty that is pain,
he waited for the ivory girl to wake:
his last and lethal muse with history ahead,
whips in her hair, and from her ribs

to find her breasts, two threads of trembling jet
from the titanic spider he'd emblazoned down her back.

The Pains of Sleep

She throws a gold ax at him.
There is a railing. She jumps it
like a rickety troubadour. Below,
a platform, slick and black.
he sheds her armor for the end.

In the dark above
he beams a bit,
anxious, spousal.

He should have willed her
mottled trout and woodland, all
she could have craved before,
crossing the studded quiver straps
between her ruddy breasts—

He watches, light mouth
filled with fluid, as she sinks.
The coda of the Niebelungs
whines through the mast and nervous
stir of plankton in the wake
as her blood-marbled body falls
through slow-motion witnesses of all her life
and far from the blue pity of his gaze
enters, past the ship's glide.

To Gustavus Adolphus in Basic Training

Where in the whole night air
are you, with a haversack,
damp boots, perhaps a flare?
Are you tonight on exercise
on foot, tilting the compass
up to the night's anxious glow?

I live on a street of practice
bells, civilian false alarms,
the blacks who've served. I fear the theft
in a three-quarters furnished room
of something other than a chair,
something wry, and quietly concealed.

Where in the broad oat plain
do you have lunch—in a landscaped

shrub? atop a spur? Do you
have to rub your face against
your hand when the tawny wind
rakes across your chest, your pack?

I need, it seems, to question you,
to ask you how you read these racks
of coded sunlight from the shades,
to ask you to decipher—you:
how you'd look to me when I
can't see, how you'd think of gestures

you don't note, how you'd really
see yourself as I could see you
(not knowing yet what I think of all this
since you refuse). It is the mutual
devotion, that I miss, of circumstance
to method, of the method to the purposive.

I counted ten on the underside
of your arm; in portrait, spreading
plums above your ribs. The next time
I expect ten fresher purple
marks beside your knees, from grasping
fictive ropes, in fierce conditions.

Reading during Marriage

Comic the drawl of small rain
down the wavering windows
poorly fitted to their sills.
Winter sees us reconciled,
lamp lights absurdly golden
pouring their slow pools across
nap, binding, and fluted shade.
We each have a book to read
and laugh at the odd moment.

All countries are implied here
in the dusk between covers,
Russia at night and Ireland
by moonlight—Dostoievski,
Bowen. Roubles the color
of the rainbow will obtain,
in Cork up in the hot eaves
of the stone manor, the dress
ancestral that your double
wore. Brought to it by instinct,
iridescent, powerful
mirror gratuitously
reflecting what you can want
against the longing it cost,
you smile into your shadow.
Women. Best writers, best wives,
devisers of that twilight
toward which all things tend.

Mortally tired but nothing
wasted I see the fair sweep
(as you depart the carriage
wheel scoring her muff with snow)
of my face in your regard:

this no older than I am,
that no longer discouraged.

Asked to Recall a Moment of Pure Happiness

The bed's height is one reason
for floating. It is near noon.
Again you have overslept.

On the Hotel Belvedere
a triangle of sunlight

bites across the reddish bricks,
but in the alley's camera
the bulk are in blue shadow
that glints off the iron grille
of your fire stairs, or cages.
This happy imprisonment
makes no sense, yet is not false.
Your life is starting over.

Traffic moans from the other
room that floods with yellow day.
The little hallway of shelves
between that dazzling ceiling
and this murkier, blue one
fills with a loose corolla,
ambiguous and humming.

Life, day, shadowy iron
and sun, whispering taxis,
heat at the end of summer
raising a mist on your skin,
Eager Street, Charles, Mt. Vernon,
Biddle, St Paul—in their arms
you float into your future.

Looking Back

You would not speak of what was not right here.
What grieved me when I died was that
dying was the note you could not hear.
You would not speak. Of what was not, right here
(singing on the threshold of the year)
or in the night that came, to come—that
you would not speak of. What was not right here,
what grieved me when I died, was that.

The Quest
—for Mary Etta Knapp

Like an old duchessa who has talked all night
whom the Republic's leaders have forgotten,
Venus is guided up the dim cone of rooms,
still glowing through her empty outpost
alone among already vanished stars.

The sun increases in her wake.
Putting off his moony Dutch enamel
for direct Baroque, the young retainer
hales up in repeated ormolu
a cold, new wind in the clicking trees.

At the corner of the garden
as that surprised vague rash
on a nearly white Bosc
grows into smiling russet
from far enough away,
an adolescent beech
thrusts his pride of bristling opal
from the matted lawn,
blushing when you look back
from the verge.

But among that litter of leaf as the gate closes
you have seen, between the bony poplars there, and
        there,
a few bright charms tied in yellow to the twigs
to tell you in the blowing forest where you should have
        turned.

Harry Humes

Winter Weeds

1983

Harry Humes's most recent collection of poems, *The Bottomland*, was published in 1995 by the University of Arkansas Press, which also published his *Ridge Music* in 1987 and *The Way Winter Works* in 1990. He lives near Lenhartsville, Pennsylvania, with his wife and daughter.

The Man Who Carves Whales

All summer long out of pine
and birch the great whales flow
from my knife, blue and finback,
sperm whale, right, and sei
with flukes easy as smooth runs
of deep water. I work hours
on the strange heads, the mouths
full of baleen plates or ivory teeth

Other days when my knife
goes dull or quiet with loss,
I read of their convoluted brains
and half-ton hearts, can hear the songs
deep in the latitudes
of scrimshaw and krill.

I keep them close to my hands,
polish them, and all around me
the season moves toward Scammon Lagoon,
the Chuckchi and Bering Seas.
I think of them there
running out of breath, drowning
with the New World, with cities and faces
that have no need for the breach of mystery.

When I open my knife again
I see in the wood a moment,
the end of shapes I must carve my way into
over and over

Savage Remembers a Horse

All is not well. . . .
This evening in the upper fields,
a pheasant drummed the air. . . .

I was thinking of the way
the night came flowing down
between the antlers of the deer.

I was standing up to my waist
in the rattling weeds, tired
of being civilized. It was autumn,

and I could see how it would end:
the return of the blazing horse,
the imagined ride across the world,

the sparks flung star-profusely
out of order, into wildness, flowing
from the great chest, muscled, racing,

huge against the smallness of the world.
And my hand, light on the reins,
purely in touch with moves

remembered by my deepest parts.
Such wild companionship controls
the flaming failure of the leaves.

I know how the self is lost in air,
so I will have it this way always:
at the heart of the world is a beast.

There's a field, noisy with weeds;
there's my blood, that rider, primitive,
freer than anything ever before.

The Rain Walkers

One day soon from out of the fevers of brown lips
and the cracked mud of ponds they will come
suddenly around corners up blacktop roads

into the dirt lanes of farms they will see only rivers
and hear near their wrists and temples the tap tap of rain
on windows and spouts against the hollows of shagbark
and walnut they will remember the parched rooms
the inches of thirst the sun turning their blood
into the rattle of yellow corn leaves

                         One day soon
they will come to the meadows the old orchards
to the round wooden tables of breakfast the breasts
of their women will shine through damp blouses
Even at midnight as they walk past the white marks
of old floods and driftwood near pilings of bridges
you will hear the drizzling syllables
falling everywhere around them the sweet dust
rising like light like mint leaves as you sleep then
as you wake in the predawn sorrow as you wonder
at such puddles near faces at what they are saying
at the way your own voice your own hands suddenly fill
with them the softness beneath them the earth at last wet

The Spheres of October

What do I remember here in October,
having gone out after dark for carrots
and then to have cut the potatoes and bread?
The fire cracks with rounds of hickory and locust,
the night with starscape of ridge and field.
All day long there was a steady rain.
Now there's most of a moon and the smell
of beasts. . . .
            Is it a way of sleeping
I have forgotten, or the laws of motion,
of grass and light bending off their lines?
Newton knew it well, this memory
that comes to the skin like ground fog,
this nostalgia of all things to become spheres.

Reading Late by a Simple Light

All day long there'd been windows to fix,
the shed to clean, last tomatoes to pick.
Toward dusk, he walked the fields
to the abandoned orchard and pond.
A neighbor's dog howled at the passing geese.
The green heron hunched on a dead limb.
Near the small stream he stopped
and watched the water whirl around roots,
past the muskrat's hole, and past his sight.
He thought of fishing line and lures,
a rod arced along an April sky.
But here, here were the yellows
of evening primrose and cornfields. . . .

He would think about it all later,
as he sat reading by a simple light,
of how it had entered his eye quietly,
of how, by the water and the heron's dark hunch,
he had felt the first chilly edge,
the first snowflake touch his cheek,
and felt again the steady puzzle
of all the old planet's motions.

The Muskellunge

I'd walked past the store, stopped, then drifted back
to where the window bulged with reels,
tapered fishing line, lures, and hooks.
And since it was November, shotgun shells,
red hunting hats, gloves, and one stuffed owl.
So having seen that old familiar country
rising up, I went in with some veiled hope
of finding there some object, something
apart from the wind and the threat of snow.

I moved between the glassed-in shelves,
inspecting this or that device, and once
considered buying a knife with twenty blades
(to slash, punch, scale, or open cans of beer),
but I said no, and left it, moving among
the fathers, sons, salesmen, feeling somehow
out of place, as if they knew I'd come
with no good reason, making moves
I'd made too long ago, forgetting all
except the blood-deep feel of them.
And so it was I came to where the muskellunge lay,
its heart drowned in some cold play.

There I stopped and felt its river wetness
on my face; saw its belly white as sleet;
and eyes unfathomable, as though a stone
would sink in them in spirals out of time.
Even lying dead it seemed to move,
weaving with the river, muscular and tough,
beyond the dirty floor, the store, the stares.

And I thought of that great river,
Susquehanna, like a dark vein
flowing through this afternoon of grief;
past the fishermen by fires huddled
on gray banks; past the faded patchwork farms;
and by the deer-and-fox-quick forest.

And for a time I saw that fish rage,
with its violent cargo of teeth,
across the tangled waters of the world,
prepared to rip the right whale of the flesh
to shreds, the minnow of the bone to dust.

Ah muskellunge,
if you could tell what water weaves itself
around you now, or what dark hunger drove

you to embed yourself on a barbed world,
or why in death your lines precisely
arch like sky down to the river's edge,
then I could tell why, on a bitter day,
I felt your dead heart like the April sun
break up the jam of sorrow's ice.

Outside in the air, as I left the store,
some rhythm picked up and carried
through the flakes inexorable waves
that broke down this long afternoon
like heavy swirls that some great fish
would cause in shallows, just before
it turns and glides inevitably away.

The Coyote in the Orchard

Now in the year's cold closing
with the trees emptied of everything,
my blood leans to moonlight

on deep fur, to the pointed face
already wet with mice.
I can almost hear it moving

along the slippery margins of towns.
Maybe a twig snaps beneath a paw
as it passes on legs steady as old trails

along the Kittatinny Ridge
to Owl's Head, the North Lookout.
It must move with the slow burn

of winter pushing up the land.
As the night glitters high on its stars,
I lean to the passing shape,

to the tight hold of the dark,
to the eyes flashing like small dawns,
to a way of remembering

here in the year's cold closing
the clear spoor across the air,
the shadowy skin of edges and frost.

Hawk Mountain in the Fog

The year has come down to these rocks.
Not even the trees can make it out of the fog.
Last night my dog turned wolf and howled
with the wind in his blood,
but here all is silent.
The trails clog with the unseen.
Over there somewhere is Owl's Head,
the North Lookout; a month ago the mountain
turned buoyant with migration.
Now the hawk of the mind holds its limb,
steels its eye, steadies its hunger
in dark places where it waits out the fog.
Resisting this lonely afternoon,
or even loving it, our hands part everything
slowly, one lost season after another.

Wesley McNair

The Faces
of Americans in 1853

1984

Wesley McNair lives in Mercer, Maine. He has
received two Fellowships from the National Endow-
ment for the Arts and grants from the Rockefeller,
Fulbright, and Guggenheim Foundations. His most
recent volume of poetry is *My Brother Running*
(Godine).

Small Towns Are Passing

Small towns are passing
into the rearview
mirrors of our cars.
The white houses
are moving away,
wrapping trees
around themselves,
and stores are taking
their gas pumps
down the street
backwards. Just like that
whole families picnicking
on their lawns tilt
over the hill,
and kids on bikes
ride toward us
off the horizon,
leaving no trace
of where they have gone.
Signs turn back and start
after them. Packs of mailboxes,
like dogs, chase them
around corner after corner.

Mina Bell's Cows

O where are Mina Bell's cows who gave no milk
and grazed on her dead husband's farm?
Each day she walked with them into the field,
loving their swayback dreaminess more
than the quickness of any dog or chicken.
Each night she brought them grain in the dim barn,
holding their breath in her hands.
O when the lightning struck Daisy and Bets,

her son dug such great holes in the yard
she could not bear to watch him.
And when the baby, April, growing old
and wayward, fell down the hay chute,
Mina just sat in the kitchen, crying "Ape,
Ape," as if she called all three cows,
her walleyed girls who would never come home.

Hair on Television

On the soap opera the doctor
explains to the young woman with cancer
that each day is beautiful.

Hair lifts from their heads
like clouds, like something to eat.

It is the hair of the married couple
getting in touch with their real feelings for the first time
on the talk show,

the hair of young people on the beach
drinking Cokes and falling in love.

And the man who took the laxative and waters his
        garden
next day with the hose wears the hair

so dark and wavy even his grandchildren are amazed,
and the woman who never dreamed minipads
could be so convenient wears it.

For the hair is changing people's lives.
It is growing like wheat above the faces

of game show contestants opening the doors
of new convertibles, of prominent businessmen opening
their hearts to Christ, and it is growing

straight back from the foreheads of vitamin experts,
detergent and dog food experts helping ordinary
     housewives discover

how to be healthier, get clothes cleaner, and serve
dogs meals they love in the hair.

And over and over on television the housewives,
and the news teams bringing all the news faster
and faster, and the new breed of cops winning the fight
against crime, are smiling, pleased to be at their best,

proud to be among the literally millions of Americans
     everywhere
who have tried the hair, compared the hair, and will
     never go back
to life before the active, the caring, the successful,
     the incredible hair.

The Bald Spot

It nods
behind me
as I speak
at the meeting.

All night
while I sleep
it stares
into the dark.

The bald spot
is bored.
Tired of waiting
in the office,

sick of following me
into sex.

It traces
and retraces

itself,
dreaming
the shape
of worlds

beyond its world.
Far away
it hears the laughter
of my colleagues,

the swift sure
sound of my voice.
The bald spot
says nothing.

It peers
out from hair
like the face
of a doomed man

going blanker
and blanker,
walking backwards
into my life.

The Thugs of Old Comics

At first the job is a cinch like
they said. They manage to get the bank teller
a couple of times in the head and blow the vault door
        so high
it never comes down. Moneybags line the shelves
inside like groceries. They are rich, richer
than they can believe. Above his purple suit the boss

is grinning half outside of his face.
Two goons are taking the dough in their arms
like their first women. For a minute nobody sees
the little thug with the beanie is sweating drops
the size of hotdogs and pointing
straight up. There is a blue man flying
down through the skylight and landing with his arms
crossed. They exhale their astonishment
into small balloons. "What the," they say,
"What the," watching their bullets drop
off his chest over and over. Soon he begins to talk
about the fight against evil, beating them half to death
with his fists. Soon they are picking themselves up
from the floor of the prison. Out the window Superman
is just clearing a tall building and couldn't care less
when they shout his name through the bars. "We're
           trapped!
We got no chance!" they say, tightening their teeth,

thinking, like you, how it always gets down
to the same old shit: no fun, no dough,
no power to rise out of their bodies.

The Last Peaceable Kingdom
(painted by Edward Hicks in 1849)
—for Don and Jane

*By recreating his beautiful animal dream he was able to forget
the elusiveness of his ideal in the world, to erase his despair. If
individual men could not transcend their weaknesses and live
happily together, the animals he imagined could.*
                    — "Animals in American Art: Edward Hicks"

Mostly they recall nothing. The bear just
nudges the cow and feels foolish

to be wearing claws and the young lion
continues on his way with the child. Still
there are times the leopard remembers.
Behind his tranquil eyes he sees
himself running somewhere out of his body.
And there are times the wolf lifting his fine
brown head can hear a scream
that seems to come from his own throat. Yet
it is quiet here and in the light
beyond them Penn rises with Indians
as if he were their thought. Nearby the ox
the old lion forgets that he is doomed
to browse the luminous hay forever.

Where I Live

You will come into an antique town
whose houses move apart
as if you'd interrupted
a private discussion. This is the place
you must pass through to get there.
Imagining lives tucked in
like china plates, continue driving.
Beyond the landscaped streets,
beyond the last colonial gas station
and unsolved by zoning,
is a road. It will take you
to old farmhouses and trees
with car-tire swings.
Signs will announce hairdressing
and nightcrawlers.
The timothy grass will run beside you
all the way to where I live.

Jane O. Wayne

Looking Both Ways

1985

Jane O. Wayne lives in St. Louis. Her poetry has appeared in many magazines, including *Poetry*, *Iowa Review*, *Ploughshares*, *The Massachusetts Review*, and *Poetry Northwest*. James Tate selected her most recent collection, *A Strange Heart* (Helicon Nine), to receive the Marianne Moore Poetry Prize.

Lapsing

When she stops us on the street
the white hair is what we see first,
the careful set and comb of it,
and then the three keys
strung around her neck on a shoelace,
the winter coat, the bare legs.

She can't say how many streets it's been,
how many cracks in the pavement,
look-alike doors.
Her own house she misplaces
like a pair of gloves, then just as absently
pulls out her name

as if she's had it all along
like that handkerchief in her coat pocket,
her address, too, where a man answers
tired of it—
this old woman losing herself
the way he might a pen or pencil.

She may be off the streets now
but she's still loose in our minds.
There's no forgetting her,
no hanging up on her threat
in the middle of the night,
no putting her off like a bad debt.

Outside

This sycamore when I come close
loses its birds.
The air's confused with flapping.

I'm the misfit in this garden,
like a housecat that climbs a tree
and can't get down.

Green leaf, green caterpillar,
where's my place? The lawn is spongy,
the brick ledge slippery with moss,

and puddles occupy the lawn chairs.
I'd call, but the dog won't come.
He's lapping water from a bowl of mud.

A branch rattles in the sycamore.
A nervous ripple runs along the privet's spine.
So what if the squirrels watch all my moves.

Hard plums, hard peaches,
apples still too small—
I won't need an alibi.

In the Woods

Out here, it all happens so fast:
the frozen pond opening one eye for the dog,
the man with a stick appearing
on the edge of the ice—lying down,
stretching himself out like a lifeline
on the hellish pool, trying with the stick
to fetch that Cerberus
from the underworld

until the barking
then the bobbing in the water stops,
until there's nothing more to see—the dark pupil
in the glassy eye is empty—

nothing more to hear except that stick
dropping on the ice. The woods
around the pond resume the silence
of a book closed on a myth.

With Solitude

"The secret of a good old age is simply an honorable pact with solitude."
> —*Gabriel García Márquez*

If I stare too long
the dregs congeal in the bottom of this cup.
Maybe the brindled cat holds me prisoner.

Sometimes a week can pass.
I don't go outside. I keep my secrets to myself,
let dirt accumulate beneath my nails.

Always the same chair,
until the stuffing sags, the pink upholstery thins.
The damage is a perfect fit, my image in intaglio.

And in my lap, the cat curls.
I feel the warmth through my skirt,
on one side of my face, the heat of the lamp.

Tail arched, the cat leaves the room.
Nothing moves
except the darkness in the hall.

Outnumbered by the minutes,
I hold my own with weak tea.
Sipping. Sipping.

I can outstare the night, the winter too,
outlive these teeth if I have to.
Already bare-boned stems show on the asparagus-fern.

Its thin leaves curl on the carpet,
like old hair, dry and colorless.
Adding water doesn't help.

Nor does the broom.
I don't have to try anymore.
Solitude is two smiles, the mirror's and mine.

At Dusk

Sometimes I stroll at dusk, just to hear
cutlery clinking on china, strangers

stacking dinner dishes, laughter.
This is the season for open windows,

for barefoot girls shrieking over the lawns
after lightening bugs. And in a jar

the greenish-yellow lights
severed from the flies are still flickering.

When I come close, they all glance away.
I must be one of those,

a hag caught humming under her breath
the same song over and over.

A man approaches hauling a leash.
His shapeless dog scrapes along the pavement.

Without slackening, the man turns
slightly toward the curb and spits.

In the street a boy heaves a football.
Another misses it. The distance

is the game between the players, between the head
and hand, between this moment and another.

Recurring Symptoms

Disease comes at noon.
When I lean against the southern wall
I'm one with the shadow.

Some days I am afraid to move.
If the wind stirs
the nest sways high in the birch.

I rest on the ground
reading from my palms
the short-lived creases of the grass.

My nights grow dizzy
near the water.
I can almost hear the splashing.

Every morning I wipe the dust
from my eyes.
I wind my watch.

To the Uninvited

Her party, dear,
is the same party that we read about:
twelve golden plates in the palace,
thirteen fairies in the kingdom.
There's never enough to go around.
Someone makes a list,

someone else is uninvited.
A wish turns to a curse, a fairy
to a witch—you know the rest:
the pricking rage,
the whole court in its spell,
a century behind a thorn hedge
to sleep it off,
to let a kiss through. Remember, too,
taking Sleeping Beauty's side,
slighting the witch so willingly?
Such an easeful story then—
nothing cautionary, nothing real,
none of us in it.

By Accident

Because I brought him here
I hold his hand
while the surgeon cleans his leg,
a boy I hardly know, a child
my daughter's age. Years ago
a black nurse held
my white hand in a hospital and I
squeezed then just as he does now
a stranger never thanked
never forgotten.

I know how it happens,
how pain softens us as easily
as habit hardens, how
we meet now and if we meet again
we both avert our eyes,
the boy and I,
as from the gash itself,
the white seams gaping on the raw red,
we turn away. Often I think we can,
given half a chance, love anyone.

Autumnal Equinox

While I dry the dinner dishes
she crayons on my stationery,
a get-well card. She asks without looking up
how the leaves know when to fall
but doesn't listen.

She seals the envelope on the subject,
rubs it with her small palm for emphasis
and pushes it aside.
She doesn't want to know about the equinox
or her grandmother

just as I don't want to hear
these plates clattering or know
in this dusk between my child's innocence
and my mother's illness—what my hand
knows first on the cold ribs of this radiator.

The way today is equal to tonight
my life now must be equal
to its dark time; in this kitchen,
at this sink, love must be the axis
that our years spin around.

Shirley Bowers Anders

The Bus Home

1986

Shirley Bowers Anders received her B.A. from
Salem College in Winston-Salem, North Carolina,
and an M.F.A. degree from Bennington College. She
studied writing with A. R. Ammons and George
Garrett. At various stages of her career, Anders
taught at the University of North Carolina, Greens-
boro and at the University of Wisconsin, Fox Valley.
She died in August 1994.

Poems for James Gilmore Bowers
1888-1959

If I forget you,
let my right hand forget her cunning.
If I do not remember you,
let my tongue cleave
to the roof of my mouth.

1. My Father Never Got to Russia

He was a man who never changed his mind.
But someone told me: young and burly,
full of the daily endless railroad run,
full of the harridan dependent mother,
expensive sisters, one brother dead
of railroad cars, another gone
with drink, bung full
of sisters' husbands, Jesus!
Daddy left, for Murmansk, Leningrad,
wherever all that clacking track
the old czar laid down with his ruler
cut the steppes in half. Lincoln Steffens
said the future worked there.
He meant to see it.

Got just as far as New York City.
Next thing anybody knew,
here was Big Bull-Necked Gilly back again
among the ties. Nobody ever learned
what turned him round
and coaxed him home to all the yokes.

2. Sweatband Poem

Home from the train on Sunday
and no churchgoer, he wore his old felt hat
jammed to the eyebrows,
clean bib overalls, silk socks,
high-button work shoes already out-of-date.
He sat on he porch. Picture it:
1940, a righteous socialist,
feet to banister, straight chair tipped
to the stretch of his legs, his rare leisure.
When my brother wired that chair,
when he hid round the corner
with the hand-cranked generator Daddy saved
for Christmas lights, when my brother
ground the current out,
its whirr shot our father godless,
harmless, stung, swearing by nothing
through his house. Dadblame,
he hollered, running in railroad shoes,
chasing the child whose science
turned him to a lightning rod.

6. His Intelligence, Our Education

From cinder dirt by railroad sidings,
from low land near the boarding house
at the far end of his run,
he dug wildflowers:
two kinds of jewelweed,
columbine, wild geranium, sundrop,
trillium, star jasmine.

From somewhere he brought home
for us to learn them
plaques of different woods,
veneer chips of the various oaks, maples;
yellow poplar, no true poplar, but the tulip tree,

he was careful we should know that;
pines, so many; ash;
plaques slung on string like paint-hue samples;
I remember their textures, their dry odors; cedar;
I remember names, but would not know the woods;
what did we learn? Not what he taught.

He brought home rocks.
Clusters of quartz crystals. Mica, in sheets.
Bauxite by the lump: white streak in red sponge.
Bauxite powder smooth from the mill's battering,
so we could see what happened to it.
Fool's gold, and the real thing in its ore,
blue vein through pudding stone.

We sunk the wildflower roots in the back garden
by the black walnut's trunk.
The wood chips lay in his glass-front bookcase
with *Ten Days That Shook the World.*
Those rocks stayed on the fancy tray on the sideboard
(a wedding gift, dead butterflies and milkweed tassels
rotting under glass edged with twisted raffia) for years.

7. Memorial Day Weekend, 1943

Still wearing his conductor's hat,
hot with virtue after half his run,
his train in on time, due home tomorrow,
he pitched right from the rocker
to the boardinghouse veranda floor,
lay there till they moved him
to the parlor sofa. He waked,
talky, through night-train coupling noises,
steam emissions, whistle shrieks.
They hauled him back like freight.
That road ran by his track.
Braced for the effort, he sat high
in the swaying ambulance, eyes avid at the window

for cinder banks, for the passing train,
for wild geraniums pushing pink and weak
through soot. Insistent, he talked, fluent.

Home, they carried him to bed.
He said "I'll walk." They said "No."
He slept that night.

He lay still for the doctor, heard his wife:
"They called me all the way to Wadesboro.
But it's not so bad. See,
it's not so bad. He's better.
Aren't you better, Gilly?"
He heard the answer, "Bed rest,"
heard his wife say "Thank you," listened

as, talking, they left the silent patient

poking the plates and crevices
of his skull, peeping through gelatin,
weighted, tongue gone to stone
between night and that morning.

11. A Souvenir from a Visit to the City

Your Russian peasant jumping jack is antique
now, in his red slouch cap, gold tunic,
wood britches with their carved stylized folds.
His beard juts springy as ever,
his hands, palms out in the priest's
gesture of blessing, jiggle, lift, drop;
his boots kick like any other
jumping jack's. You bought him new
in New York City. Did you say
he is Ukrainian? Do I imagine that?
How did you know? He hangs from a pin
in your granddaughter's bedroom.
When he needed new strings, I matched

the old knots, precisely. You would be proud.
He makes your great-grandson laugh.

12. Easter Saturday, City Cemetery,
Winston-Salem, North Carolina

We scrub the stones, ready
for another Easter, my daughter,
my grandson, and I, with no clear notion
why we do this thing. Nicholas, who is small
and tires soon of any amusement, washes slapdash
at the smallest grave, under the forsythia border,
an infant second cousin. With an ice pick
my daughter digs soot from the letters
of my father's mother's name. I tend my father.

This bird-dropping stain is green verging to plum.
I wonder what the minerals are,
what chemicals, how they combined
to make these colors I bleach out.
I have no sense of dirt.
Detergent foam from my brush bristles
runs white into the mud that is red
from iron in our soil. I see the soil
suck moisture, trace of foam
alter the earth it enters.

We are done here and my grandson is restless.

I gather our tools.

To whom do we minister? Our dead
were ready, I think. These motions we make
not for them, people beyond being people,
beyond needing anything. Not one wanted
a last wish. Not yet beyond anything, I wish
for them to be allowed not to rise,
not to rise, to be leached

free of all they were, in their integrity
held steady, like ducks in a press, under clean stones.

I turn to the car. Nicholas must be carried;
his mother wears him on her shoulder,
whispers to him. The easy freight
of the bucket swings by its bail
from her free hand. Glancing back,
I see her lean into the wind
as the bucket swings, as she follows, as her son dozes.

Her Memory of Early Winter

Washbowl: clay with white glaze
on the white stand. Water
under a membrane of crystals.
The lace curtain blown aside,
cool to the hand; cold air,
the windowsill, its blunt curve,
its raised sash beside the bed.
Snow granular on her pillow slip,
pricking her cheek as they waked.
These she remembers. Mornings.
How the sisters shared
that sleepy chill.

Old and insular, she fingers
white tatting
edging old linen, old consciousness
swimming against the stream:
widowhood, births, marriages,
merging in the single, sisterly
and distant, beckoning cold.

The Bus Home

Somewhere on the way back
in the dark between Richmond and Lynchburgh,
in the smelly Greyhound air-conditioned chill
slick and stale as cheap hair oil,
a stranger will astonish you,
smiling, spreading his jacket over
your shoulders, your cold upper arms,
as you lie—invisible, you thought—
in the corner of window and rough seat back.

You will know but will not trust for years:
something in your condition touched him.

You will sleep better, warmly. Sleep
is what you need as you are driven
back to what you ran from.

Starting from the Port Authority terminal,
somehow through New Jersey. Then
the long black stretch south
from State Road Delaware with its cafeteria
where you ate lime jello. You roused
at Washington. Between gluey eyelids,
through tinted glass, you glimpsed
the tumescent Capitol and the Monument rising
lime-green, livid as neon beyond
your nearer vision, accidents
of wreckage. Borne on down the road
you doze, happy when you sleep, Fortune's
child. Doomed one, blessed one. Not
till you have finished failing may you prophesy.

Nancy Schoenberger

Girl on a White Porch

1987

Nancy Schoenberger teaches creative writing at The College of William & Mary. She is the author of *The Taxidermist's Daughter*, a chapbook from Calliopea Press, and *A Talent for Genius: The Life and Times of Oscar Levant*, published by Villard Books and co-written with her husband, the poet Sam Kashner.

Cypresses

Pulled by the roots from a hot Southern town
where we unfolded like geraniums, grafted
to the icy bayside of Northern wilderness—
fast cars, fast girls, fast tongues!—
we fasted till your asthma kicked up, the frigid air
sliced through the bellows of your lungs.
At knife point once you gave up your allowance.
I dyed my hair and applied lipstick with a vengeance
and let the boys come, I didn't care.
You were summer's own fair-haired boy.
You would rather be funny than smart. All night
at your blonde violin, playing the same tune over again,
getting it right, the ode to joy you understood
at fourteen and finally got right, all of us
yelling at you to *shut up*. At seventeen you went under,
went into the trees in your new Triumph. I've gone
back South once or twice, though you never will.
The last time I sat at Cafe du Monde
I watched the pigeons swirl like a cape
around Jackson's horse, in Jackson's square,
sky gilded like a rococo sky, a place
like any other place, to tell the truth—
perhaps more pink. I went to Pierre Part
and the labyrinthine channels of water,
now empty of significance. Near Audubon
where the silted river slides to the sea
with its cargo of Northern sorrows, I saw cypresses
hanging their hair in park's charred light.
Now you come to me in dreams and tell me *it's too cold*
though the long roots of the trees wrap you round
and winds still blow warm from the Gulf.

Perdita

*"Your girlhood was finished, your sorrows were robing you
with the readiness of woman."*

—Derek Walcott

Adrift in New Orleans in a yellow dress
in yellow October, between jobs, boyfriends,
friends, and schools, in the first, fresh

heat of denial, slipping between the deepened
shadows of the live oaks on St. Charles
toward the Audubon Park seal pool, whose deep end

is shrouded, past the stone halls
with their museum of fishes: garfish
and shoepick, and the lawless

and terrible snakehouse (languish-
ing anaconda, limp coils of snakeflesh)—
like a spoon rattling a dish

she strode through the brilliant mesh
of shadows on Greek-copied statues, the rays
of spiders' threads dress-

ing the larger web of trees, and the spray
off the seals' impossibly sleek backs
(oblivious, uncle-faced!);

laughed at the seals and the fact
she could go in any direction, could whirl
across the miniature tracks

of the toy railroad she rode as a girl
through the lugubrious oaks of Audubon.
Who would have said, in that new world,

she would go home and, thoroughly undone,
cut off her hair like Jeanne D'Arc,
but without the angels? It had begun:

she left the park
and its paradise of statues,
threw out her summer dresses, locked

in some weird penance. But sometimes it rose,
it opened like a gate left ajar
for a whole morning. Lies?

Fictions? Something stirs,
as when Giulietta Masina in the old film
is hypnotized by a traveling huckster:

the swilling paesanos are hushed, the realm
of the theater changes: Look! She's a girl of sixteen.
She dances, and in her arms

are her first flowers. On winter evenings,
Perdita, just think of it. Go back to the park.
The spell is broken, but the statues are living.

Girl on a White Porch

Where do they go, the young boys, glass
splintering their hearts? Called back?
It was the same river: car overturned,
his yellow hair covered the rocks like grass.
Somebody held him, he would not get up.
Who was that girl who held her brother,
her blue dress and the evening finished?

In those days the shell road followed the river.
Alone on the porch swing, among the wisteria:
the girl and her brother.

And the trees heavy with oranges,
and the heat on their limbs like a hand
through the hosannas of the tree frogs.

Rain settles on the elm. A Keatsian mood
contaminates the lawn, tells the tale
of their innocence, the wet streets
shining like licorice. Because in poems
we weep for ourselves, in sepia weather
that spreads like a river.

When we are through with nostalgia,
will the two halves, memory and desire,
finally call them back?
No more a summer of hothouse flowers,
girl on a white porch and all the wisteria
falling to touch her.

The Taxidermist's Daughter

Always long afternoon shadows
began leaking from tame leaves
near the plot of sunflowers, the valuable
statuary, chickens restless
as the best game cocks paired off
and started their dance,
father his work

restoring the draggled animals
that had gathered all morning
in the pine loft above the house,
from the wild Atchafalaya,
and Arkansas turkeys,
their Indian headdresses
limp and smeared and asking
for new life. The squirrel
that one day would fly again

in the showcase, and again
in my dreams, in dream-walks
through the glass house, fly
next to the lynx
and the rare white fox.

And the tamed dogs eyeing their masters,
and the fighting wild rooster,
my sunflower drifting over the gravel
marking the day's path. I wanted to help:

carry blood in a bucket,
order the glass eyes
from the warehouse of missing parts.
I wanted to help in your dark,
private work in the loft.

Nights the gray squirrel rattles the roof,
rubs the glass where his stuffed mate
swoons in the final leap. I can still see you
bent over your work, shucking and stitching,
fur stuck to your apron. Choose me,
father. All these years I wanted to say,
choose me, as you bent down
to put the last touch
to the beautiful wood duck.

Shiraz

Beyond the hotel grounds the rigid slaves
on pillar after pillar served their king
in stark Persepolis. I taught my sister
how to dance—my beautiful sister—as the band
downstairs began a bossa nova, sending Parisian vocals
over bored, Iranian sands. Too shy
to join the guests, we danced alone
in our hotel room, colliding and dipping

(our two left feet, our drunkenness!).
What were two women doing in Shiraz,
almost thirty, husbandless, afraid
our lives were spinning on without us, while the sky
pulled her starry *chador* across her face
night after night? Poets!
Lovers! Dancers! Where is it written
that beauty is its own reward? So what
if casual roses shed their petals
in brimming waters of the hotel pool
reflecting, as it did, the sequined band,
the air gone palpable as silk pajamas?
Dust funnels hung from heaven on the horizon
like loose threads from a slumming angel's gown.
And so, going forward, nations can
return to centuries of yoke and custom,
as in opening a passage to the future
that winds down through the bowels of Isfahan—
the seven miles of the Bazaar—
to Ali Baba's cave. The rock rolls back.
Back in the States, in malls
lit up with their goods, I'll recall
girlhood dreams of dancing by a pool
where women are admitted into heaven
and history's the fountain we began from.

Epithalamion

Let the cruel spring begin, Sweeney.
I've had too many lovers as it is,
though I think of them as husbands,
and I think of them,
but it's *me* that I remember.
As if, poised on the brink of a river,
I was part of that river. Take the Mississippi:
nearby in Murphy's Pharmacy
Van Morrison sang *brown-eyed girl*

where Manuel and I wolfed down our hamburgers.
That was Baton Rouge, and, narcissistic,
those songs were always me in my green time.

Not that all this yearn and pull is over.
Far from it: Ophelia's floating
down the Thames in her blue underthings.
Now if my lovers have married other women,
so be it: I don't care. In my best fantasy
I'm beautiful, in a rose-pink gown. It's silly,
yes, I know that—it goes on. I'm surrounded
by animals: sloe-eyed does, pigeons, cows
returned to their wild state—even giraffes—
everyone horned, hoofed, and feathered.

We form one long procession down the levee
among Exxon's refineries, like a page
out of Kipling. You're wondering what's missing
as we move along: no wedding knives,
no altar, and no one in this picture
to declare that beauty.

By Certain Rivers

But what do I remember? Colors. The cottonwood
full of pollen, swollen waters.
These images have hardened into granite
by a tin-colored river. Something about
the agreement of skin and air, sexual,
on the banks of the fathering waters, in fallen
autumn. Father's arrival on *The Constellation*
had us up all night in a waterfront park,
my sisters and I on the swings,
my brothers asleep in the sandbox. Floridian eve,
September had begun its little deaths
among the stinking leaves and sagging woods,
men in dress whites streaming through the park

like the end of the world—*the reckoning*
is coming.

        By certain rivers
women are given over to weeping;
derelicts drink alone or in pairs
to still the beautiful harpies;
by certain rivers
men loading granite onto flatbeds
feel the living resistance of granite;
runaways from the Midwest see their deaths
in the eddying waters, the cottonwood
nodding like horses; by certain rivers
boats are unloading their precious cargo—
cows, sheep, pigs; by certain rivers
we came down and the men surrounded us,
taking us in their arms, their bleached
suits glowing, all the women waving and crying
for those who were coming, those
who were going away.

Penelope Wilkinson Austin

Waiting for a Hero

1988

Penelope Austin lives with her family in the mountains of north-central Pennsylvania. She continues to write and to direct Wordworks Writing Center for Adults and Children.

Modernism

That is not my country, though I speak
as a ghost now. There forever means
forever, and there is no need for dignity
among the souls in the long processional
blurring into sky. Still, even at the fit
end of pain toward which they rode, madly,
maudits, on fast horses, in fast cars,
or unwillingly by the boxcarful,
they turn to one another with what's left:
a single perfect note held unwaveringly.
That is the eternity they believed in.
Their condition is the music of souls
stretching now and forever like the thin skin
of embarrassment they wear for absent bodies
cast off in another country left behind.

Eternal Love

Play it. The line of palms stretching along
　the blue coast, and the train's song
　　as it coasts into the station. Play
　it again. Golden grains of couscous

harden where the wine stains
　the tablecloth, beneath the fingernail idly
　　scratching at the table beneath stars, stars like
　the grains of golden sand on the beach, golden sand

ground into golden skin. Play it again.
　She's wearing a white dress, of course,
　　and sandals. His eyes go from blue to green
　to brown and back again to the sea.

Oh, the lovers come and go
　across the gilt-edged borders of Morocco.

Going Back

Gypsies came down my street in summer
    and spilled their satin ribbons, gaudy beads,
    and yards of scarves and brightly colored

remnants on the boulevard. We swarmed
    around, holding our bats and butterfly
    nets, drawn to the exotic perfume

of distant countries. Our mothers
    slipped out from behind screen doors
    and came to stand behind us, arms

around our shoulders, palms of their hands
    pressed flat against our chests, drawing
    us close against their legs. And in the late

dry breeze of August, the iceman
    heaved blocks as cold as the memory
    of winter on his tattooed shoulder. The ragman

and the scissors-grinder sang their way
    along our street. On other days
    the organ-grinder danced with his monkey

and a man with a pony photographed
    each of us in front of the houses we left.
    All this happened in the warm season

when one sweet day rolled after another
    before memory gave us something to hope for.
    Now I can't say for sure that the gypsies

came down my street more than once, though
    these days I remember waiting for them,
    as if at thirty-five, entering every city

a stranger, I could turn my feet to the past
   and still find something coming toward me,
something whose shape I know.

There is no art to wandering.

Mrs. Walker's Injunction Becomes a Desire

At Daisy's age I was initiated by an Italian
in the backseat of a Fiat. I'd begun to walk
to *il centro di Roma*, a sultry hour
away, naively oblivious to the unhealthy
urbanity of the city I'd sauntered off
to find. The blurred edges of Rome were beautiful,

but I was pursuing the clearly beautiful:
deep catacombs, curlicue friezes, Italian
inlaid marbles, and a more ancient sun's glance off
the bleached porticoes of a cloister's walk.
I abandoned my friends, who'd consumed unhealthy
pale *gelati* after a golden noon hour;

mapless, I attempted the Sistine in an hour.
The three *ragazzi* in the car were beautiful
in my estimation, with nothing unhealthy
in their flourish of inviting gestures or their Italian
colloquialisms. Why should I walk?
I accepted the ride, and the driver took off.

The boy in back went right to taking off
my dress, working the silver zipper for a Roman hour.
The "Wedding Cake" glinted on the other side of a walk.
As from under marble his whisper slid: *Com' è bella!*
Even I understood this sliver of Italian.
They say the air above the Tiber is as unhealthy

as the silver age of an empire is unhealthy.
Marble arms, more graceful than strong, fall off
or grow too languid to resist an Italian.
The Pantheon closed its doors during the hour
that Rome fell submissively under the beautiful
certainty of the hot sun slanting up the sidewalk

like a hand sculpting legs too weak to walk.
The Italians must have found my breathing unhealthy;
they dropped me at the Coliseum with a few beautiful
bending over backward kisses and drove off
in the bloom and perfume of Rome. Since that hour
I have desired everything Italian.

Faintly between the lines James wrote: "Walk off
to the Pincio, Daisy. Desire has but one unhealthy hour.
You are beautiful and . . ." The rest is in Italian.

Never *he said say jungle again*

Though all around was waste and wild,
though jewel beetles gleamed from the undersides of
       leaves,
and monkeys cried out in two syllables.

Vipers wound round the posts of the plank road at ankle
       height,
so I hardly dared look through the light arcing
on my lashes to the tangle of leaves

at the dome of trees, or beyond
the speckled patterns of leaf shadows and dark
animal forms on limbs made strong under their weight.

I hardly dare breathe or listen to the fear at least
half desire pulsing in my ears, or part my lips, dry
cracked betrayers of a moist interior where the wrong
       word

kept forming in the mucus at the back of my throat
footsteps, beetles, bird calls . . .
two beats.

We came suddenly to the door that blocked the path
a mile from the cave, closed, padlocked, jamb flanked
and overtopped by wild vegetation, vines draped

across it, cracks encrusted with moss and gray-green
         mold.
We could step down off the plank road, swing
off its railings, into the bottomless green

surge of undergrowth, wade through the tangle of vipers
and vines, and bypass the door, hand
on a heart, perhaps,

this absurd door!—
as if the rocking frame could disarm
crimson flowers, blue frogs, monkey calls,

the iridescent butterflies called Rajah Brookes,
and the dank smell of the wet clay walls
of the cave lying somewhere beyond.

He has a photograph of me standing on this side
of the door, brown as a native, eyes shocked
by the flash, hair a tangle, fingers curled

in the vines. It was taken the split second
before I discovered the lock was not fast,
before I pushed through, crossed the threshold.

I wore orchid shoes

and blue jeans with rolled
cuffs. Still today was too brilliant for me

not to notice my hands are already old.
Where I walked was so temperate my lunacy

came back. Shingled hyacinths in low relief released
their petals' tints to the sun. Hyacinths haven't begun
to show here where I live alone on Anthony Street.
A half-year ago I was ruddy and baked in the sun.

This spring I worry that the thaw will come
here and craze the last lingering snow
glazing the clay between houses on one
side of the street one day too soon no

matter how long I prolong the rime of winter,
hoping for strength, remission, a quick cure.

Richard Lyons

These Modern Nights

1989

Richard Lyons teaches at Mississippi State University. He is a recipient of a 1984 Discovery Award and a 1992 Lavan Award. His second book of poems, *Hours of the Cardinal*, was published by the University of South Carolina Press.

Burning Stars

Stick by stick, brickface
and foundation,
I've built this house, tacking down its hair.
And some nights, like this night, across the sky
a shooting star burns out
as we sit and watch it and want to know things.
Nothing conspiratorial tends toward us
except over Liquid Carbonic
the Idle Star, the Strange Star, the Lowly Star.
They all stick close
so far from us wind draws off their sticky
galactic scent.

Tonight out on the lawn
a carnival dragon filled with friends
shuffles its sequined spine of stars
and half-moons past storefronts
and alleys, each of us breathing the mothball
fire of its fabric and shouting louder
than the next, buffeting indignities
that can't change, that we are,
as meaningless chatter about work
allows the only real work
of memory—forgetting—to draw off into vapors
any evil personal enough to touch our lives
gathering again on the lawn
to say good-bye, the evening's over
when it's just begun, headlights curving
through the pepper tree and rhododendron.

Because I don't go away
I go upstairs
and place my hands like pink starfish on the window
and lower my head as if a slew of stars
were released in holding back
when the Hungry Star staggers in, intimate

as it expands my insides
where I don't live.
Will I be frightened enough to welcome it,
saying this pane of glass
is yours, you throb of light,
empty as the hullabaloo of stars is empty
even as I stand in it,
letting each of these prima donnas
touch me with its invisible dust.
As cruel and as generous
as the fire this one burns with,
let me drift separately,
a voice, a call deserted of voice.

A Season

There's a time when a child purrs on the hip
of its parent, a horse rubs
the old hickory
and the tree's bark splinters, cracks, not one drop of
          water,
no leaf.
Nothing falls, all is spent—

each whirl of wind dies & there's another
in its place. My father & I are talking money,
scum till you have it.
So I take it, bathe in it like grief, like soot
stinking up the birches along the Charles,
naa, naa, naa, every make of car.
Not one white tree.

That's why when we were six
we rode the branches down, the crack at the base
of the tree sounded like the crack of a bat
when Williams stood in.
When you're old enough

you want to stand still awhile,
not lose something each time you look.

You want to rub your father's arm
like a tarnished piece of silver,
tell him he's not looked at most things wrong
and that your fluted life never saved anyone.
You want to save his.

The Hummingbird
—to Isaac Babel

Inside the frame of the mirror
she is nude,
not an embarrassed naked body seen from the window.
Beyond the face in the mirror
is the inner life
stunned by those who again & again
kill your grandfather,
stuffing a writhing fish in his fly.
There's a hummingbird
dipping its beak in nine tiny trumpet blossoms
winding their way up the glass.
It is the kingdom of nectar
and it is this world.

Your secrecy saved you, Isaac.
The pseudonyms.
The secret hide-outs.
Once from a small farmhouse
you watched the lovely brooding edge
of nettles as a boy fell
chasing a sheepdog. He's so nearly you
your mouth fills with the surprise of stinging nettles.
You can't go running through fields
or kissing girls.

A hat slanted on her head,
the woman knows what dipping beneath the surface
of elegant prose has in store
for the burrowing Jewish boy
she senses behind her in the mirror
now that he's gone. In a small room
his secret chest of papers—
Red Cavalry, Old Odessa, "You Must Know
Everything"—overflows.

In one of the stories, women, naked to the waist,
nurse orphaned newborns.
Isaac, the women are waiting for you
to make them live.
A cry issues from a shriveled eggplant
of an infant
on the crook of an arm.

It is not your voice.

The sweet trajectory of hummingbird is vertigo.

                    *

Hummingbirds love sugar water
my lover says.
Don't feed them honey,
it will kill them.
She unbuttons her dark blouse and
unhooks her bra.

Her landscape of breasts is like milk
with two dark coins floating in it.
Though a man may think of smoke
rising from the tip of a cigarette
over two dark coins at the bottom of a glass
as all the precision he can muster,

as his last chance,
it isn't fear,
it isn't elegy that colors everything
so undependably.
Outside the cannery
children are singing a song their parents sang
when they were children.
Isaac Babel, Isaac Babel,
where are you, you little four-eyes?
Isaac Babel, Isaac Babel,
how does it feel to be alive?
I did not mean to touch the breasts.

I touched them softly as if they were not there
beating wings beneath my hands.
Cuban Emerald, Ruby Throat,
Rufous Hummingbird.
I search for you everywhere.
I wedge a piece of cheese
in the branches of a tree.
I don't know which one, one must be careful.
Hummingbirds love sugar water.
I've wedged a piece of cheese
between two crackers
to dip in your borscht,
to finish this way: two fingers
touching a breast, something on the blurred
bright arc of hummingbird.

*

This is the dove a man smashed dead
on your forehead.
This is the shrill sound of his voice: *Jew.*
These are the soldiers who hurt the air,
the snowcrust giving way beneath the cadence
of their boots. As you lean over a bowl
of something warm, steam fogs your spectacles.

The soldiers force the door,
they crack the mirror with the butt
of a rifle. You dip past the low branches & shadows,
one feather floating down.

A few days in spring
you flash blue or green,
a visitation:
across the field of stinging nettles,
across a boy's vacant scream,
beneath the distant smoke of the cannery
near the river. You feel everything
going on as before.

The men douse the dark bodies of the salmon.
They lob the entrails to the cats.
The fish are delicious
with a squeeze of lemon.
If you can get a lemon.
If at this time of year
and with considerable resources
you get your hands on one.
A lemon! Tiny eclipse.
A hummingbird whirring.
Eyelashes brush your cheek
as she kisses you.
At the barracks during drills
the recruits shout out before they, too,
gambol in the fields.

Home

Along the freeway a wax cup
circles in wind,
cars zip by snipping houses like postage stamps,
plink, plink, plink,
mad philatelist.

You pull over & from the only
Mexican take-out in South Tucson, this dream island
in America, you watch kids exchange hits of grass.
They hold it in.
A grackle they hear then see
splits seeds like vowels,
its iridescence squeezed through the eye.
The sweet lost opulence
of the eye.

Does it comfort the air it swerves through
when you're home,
the hiss & grind of the garbage truck
shaking the road & taking nothing?
A spaniel two years dead paces the fence
and you see yourself as a young child again.
Dad's two hands, the sun—
your two ass buns two peaches ripening
to stand for awkwardness, a flag.

Now before the hall mirror
your face is a planet
suffering its bodies of water,
the tensing of lineaments like Dad's eyes, Dad's
cleft chin, it isn't portrait
it's escape. Mom's in there
behind the face
the way the roots of the big old elm
endlessly revise the earth.
Why so deeply love?
Addresses escape the mailbox.

Your brother's infant crawls awhile
then wails.
Dad's doing the windows.
With an even-measured smile of thanks, love,
blame, self-blame—
with a familiar splash of gunmetal

water on the sides of the pail
he strops the glass
on the storm door.
The aluminum family L curls its tail,
an omen now that what it stood for
is lost or almost lost
and we are here.

John Repp
Thirst Like This

1990

An assistant professor of English at Edinboro University of Pennsylvania, John Repp has been the recipient of a National Endowment for the Arts Creative Writing Fellowship as well as fellowships from Yaddo and the Millay Colony for the Arts.

My Father Demonstrates Proper Form

On each of the floodlit nights when his children's Eden
became target range, my father planted himself
among a dozen novice archers, sighting time and again
down his left arm, having simultaneously dropped
his black bow down from ten o'clock and drawn
the string, speaking the while in the rumble he'd use
to marvel at his uphill string of jobs, his meeting
our mother, the beating he got for too much wine
too young, whatever he'd met of good luck or grace.
While the dogs clicked and squealed in the kitchen
and the family gazed out the back bedroom window
and volley on volley of misdirected arrows whirred,
my father, upright agent of the Fish and Game Bureau,
stood in judgment, unhounded, untaxed, unwound,
breathing the honeyed air of mastery.

If I Went There Now I Would Walk
Through the Swordgrass

and press my booted toe in the muck and squat
to see what lives in the watercress and watch
the water carry past and love my father
for standing upstream to empty his bucket
of the trout my brother and I caught the day
we loved fishing enough to forgive his wanting it
so badly. I reject all other *why*s for the two
surprises we pulled from the dawn water
and showed him who loped down the path with net,
bucket, and the way to remove a hook,
him who runs the path eternally, a net
closing round the rare, the necessary.

Trapping Minnows at Dividing Creek

Each week my brother and I set our traps,
the deerflies' thin screams
filling the gaps in the Top 40
as we waited for the minnows'

vegetable hunger to do the job.
Driving home, we thought Christ knows what,
simmering in envy, hauling bait to sell
to men gamey and idiotic

who pointed blunt fingers at feathers
and hooks and monofilament and splitshot
arranged in pseudo-scientific
configurations—*That one, that one, and,*

OK, that one so I maybe nail a king—
and in the sixty-fifth hour of another huge week
our father fiddled with the drag
on a deep-sea reel and hustled another rod,

telling us to crank it up some more,
our sweetness boiling away
as the stock diminished and built up,
as the selling went on and on and on.

Going Full-Court

Johnnie Redfern would rise above
Big Steve and dunk or fade away,
his weightless ease transfixing us
despite our need to burn him

and the other blacks we went
full-court with on Sundays

in the park our folks said
we'd never survive till the city

cleaned it up. What bodies we had
at seventeen, how true
my shot from the baseline
and what glee to hit it

over Johnnie. Strange, I recall
his lashes and thin eyebrows
most clearly. How little I knew him
or could have, though

once or twice we talked music
or maybe girls, I don't know,
but I remember wanting to say
how much I liked his moves

and the way he pissed off Big Steve
by taking all the elbows
and scoring at will, with both hands.
Basketball became the least of things

that spring, once the black kids
shut the high school down. I sat
on the heater in homeroom, watching
for my father's car, not knowing

how he'd get through the crowds,
not knowing a gang of whites
would be jumping blacks tomorrow,
or that I could open the yearbook

twenty years later and point
to the cop with his nightstick raised,
to Michelle Brown looking back at him,
her feet poised over the tar.

Elegy for Esposito

When cicadas cling
        to screens in the night
                and ring the rapid
bell of heat,
        when the time of ice
                and shadows seems
a blessed knife,
        what better thing
                than Sam in the Spruce
preaching the gospel
        of swift care, his shears tool
                of green elegance?
Praise great, guttural
        Sammy Espo, mower supreme,
                stringer of lights,
Samuel Salvatore Esposito,
        who raced home on break
                to lift his wife
from bed to toilet and back,
        who sponged and fed her,
                who piled the dead
of Iwo in sandpits, who ate
        his ration, threw the can
                in the hole, dug
in wet heat for days,
        who said *Dead is dead.*
                Do what you can.

Van Morrison Plays Pittsburgh
—for Frank Lehner

He's sworn off arenas—no more limos, finger
        sandwiches,
ritual encores, contractual riders, cocaine fandango,
all those years of *Domino! Domino! Domino!*

so Frank and I set up a date in the Back Room.
A hundr ed, hundr ed and fifty at the most.
Beer, pretzels, they'll know who Yeats is.
Sure, OK, what the hell. On the way in
from the airport, he wonders if we like
the Symbolists and what about all these
bullshit modern visions and my God what is it
with Madonna? We arrive, he meets Ellen, Ed, Judy,
Chuck, Nancy. Kevin pumps his hand *Veedon Fleece,*
what a record! No, boring, a long time ago.
The place fills, people wonder who he is,
does he have a book, where's the waiter.
Morose, fat, mumbling, Van doodles
in a red notebook, puts back a Rolling Rock fast.

Frank does the intro with a *Van the Man!* flourish—
a woman chortles *Christ, a guitar, this isn't 1961!*—
a little feedback and he's off—a short George Herbert,
a Hopkins six-liner sung in his "Crazy Love" register,
the crowd warms a bit, another Herbert, a broken-off
        Yeats
and someone yells *Donne, do some Donne!* and a group in
        the back

chants *Blake Blake Blake* and he growls growls
turns a Donne sermon into a twelve-bar blues
that rides out on two dozen satanic yodels and a held E
comely and azure enough to head Odysseus homeward

then he's into a "Sailing to Byzantium" that's better than
        Them
chunking out "Gloria" in the fueled-up Belfast wee hours
better than Fats Navarro God rest his holy embouchure
better than Holly Aretha Jackie Wilson
better than Ray Charles' autistic amnesiac howl help me
help me now come on people on on on down
by the pylons by the pylons by the *pylons*
where the lion sings in the demon night

the lion sings in the demon night
we demons laugh in the singing night
we demons laugh in the singing night

I Continue Looking

I continue looking at two Asian women
bent over versions of the Rembrandt
hung to catch the afternoon light.
Their spines stretch and turn as pencils sweep,
heads lift and quick strokes become
twin merchants. Had I said yes to the dancer
I'd have known the sound of her singlet falling
and seen the bare floor where her thinclad feet
let the rest of her down lightly, repeating
their bargain with gravity fifty times
a minute. Had I said yes I wouldn't have known
the *whoosh* of a wooden match ignited, becalmed,
raised to the first sweet Camel of the day,
nor heard the *ah* my friends bestowed
each time I did with one hand and flair
what none of them could or wanted to.

My forebears made regimental regalia in Prussia.
Suppose some ancestor Franz had indulged
every *verboten* thing and slid at last—
ridden with the usual diseases, unbathed
his entire span—into the sea within sight
of Mycenae, a death nothing less than Byronic.
What later magic would wither, what later
suffering lift, what passing moment escape
the turn, the ripple? In a moment of love
for the Dutch and beauty unaware of itself
I turn my face from chance. Isn't that one
of us there pounding a harpsichord
in the open air? May we dance?

Judson Mitcham

Somewhere in Ecclesiastes

1991

Judson Mitcham's honors include a Creative Writing Fellowship from the National Endowment for the Arts and a Pushcart Prize. His novel, *The Sweet Everlasting*, was published in 1996 by the University of Georgia Press. Mr. Mitcham is Chairman of the Psychology Department at Fort Valley State College; he also teaches creative writing at Emory University and at the University of Georgia.

The Touch
—for my mother

You stepped out the back door, drying your hands
on a plain white apron
and watching me slap the new basketball down
on the driveway's nearly flat hardpan,
unable to control it or to stall,
for long, its falling still.

You held out clean, wrinkled hands for the ball,
let it drop and caught the rise
with the fingertips, never with the palm,
allowing no sound but the ball's hollow bounce,
crouching low, either small hand
moving *with* the ball.
                                        And years later,
when the Newton County Rams came down,
like the cavalry at dawn on a few Cheyenne,
in a hot-breath man-to-man press, the best plan
was to get the ball to me. Even now,
I return to that late fall morning
when you taught me what a softer touch could do,

now to go where I needed to, never looking down.

Home

The TV's white noise
hisses me back, this first
awareness the worst one: lights on,
wine by the bed, stale cigarettes,
chicken box greasy on the Gideon,
an hour before dawn. The orange moon
on the far wall's dull watercolor
is nowhere in the lake.

I remember my father's game.
Having come from the mill,
settled in his chair, he would say
"There is something odd in the room."
Unseen, either he had hidden
something in plain sight,
pencil in a flower pot,
or changed things slightly,
setting the clock back
or taking a knob off the radio.
He knew how simple it was
and watched us, giving no clue.

When the trucker overhead slams home,
his kicked-in turquoise door
not catching, the chain on mine
rattles. I recall
there was never a prize back then.
There was only the seeing.

Explanations

A boy holds a blown-glass sparrow in his hand
and can't resist testing one finger against
a clear, fragile wing. When it gives,
the child looks up at his mother. As if
to revise what has happened, he explains:
he didn't press hard enough to snap it. The crippled
figure is to blame.
                And when Nietzsche went insane,
when he buried his bushy face deep in the neck
of a horse whipped hard in the street, of course
there was someone to haul out the photograph
of Nietzsche himself hitched up to a cart
driven by the woman he had loved, the young
Salome wielding a whip.
              I remember

Jesus' explanation to his puzzled disciples
of his speaking in parables. Otherwise, he said,
the heathen would understand too, and they
would also be saved. I have always believed
Jesus had a zany sense of humor.
                                    Consider
the way we are taught and defeated, at once,
when a thought angles back on itself,
as when Plato alleges that Socrates lies
with every single word from his mouth, and then
Socrates owns up, holding, with a smile,
that Plato has spoken the truth.
                                    I recall
my son and his best friend, each one lost
in his own loud monologue, rolling their battered
matchbox cars down the driveway.
My son said, "History can start any time."

And his friend fell silent, appearing to ponder
how history is born,

then shook his head yes,
as though he had understood fires and freak wrecks,
leukemia and early, slow death well enough
to start off walking down the hill, not saying
just anything he happened to think of.

About Women

Who is more foolish than the poor man
who tries to give his son the honest truth
about women?
                    When the boy is thirteen,
the man thinks back to how the world had to change,
how its giving curves began to fill him up,
and he wants to tell his son what it is
he has learned since then, what women
might mean in his life.

So he tells the boy Paul was surely wrong
when he said to the Corinthians
if a man could get by, not touching a woman,
that was good. He relates how Freud
died, still baffled by females. He pulls in
Darwin to explain why everyone turns
to watch a certain girl walk by.
                      And he talks
of Saturday mornings, when the sun slants in
through the bedroom window,
how his wife comes warm into his arms
to share the way the dust luxuriates in light,
to lie there and listen to the house as it settles,
to the rustling of children in the next room,
and to drift back, together.
                    But he thinks
of something he will keep to himself:
his desire for a woman at the beach last year.
She was old, slightly bent, not beautiful.
Her housedress trailed through the foam, gaped open
to the waist.
              He is puzzled, uneasy,
remembering his daughter
in the mornings, how he finds her, tightly curled,
shivering, the quilt kicked off. How she wakes
facing any wall, turned at random, as if spun
like a bottle, unaware, though she has dreamed.

Driving Home from the Clinic

On the narrow back road to Monroe, after rain,
the air was a bittersweet tea
of mayweed mixed with the creek, wild onion, and pine,
the freshly turned earth like a root split open,
then held to the nose.

I drove home slowly, with the windows rolled down,
and I listened to the hush of the tires

on the damp asphalt,
felt the patches of cool air washing my arm,

saw a farmhouse lighted by a single yellow bulb
and drifting far out in a field
as dark as the bottom of a lake, while the clouds
to the southeast blossomed with lightning.
                                        God,
it was all of this, even
the smell of a polecat killed on the road
mingled with the wild sweet olive, this
and the news,
that compelled me to know, for the first time,

that I want to grow old,
to entertain grandchildren, telling true stories
that surprise them at the end,
stories of things long past, yet to happen.
To be able to say:

The night it all started, there was jasmine
floating on the air.
There was mica in the wet road, glistening. Cicadas
had remembered how to sing.

Sunday Evenings

Sunday mornings seemed wrong for the soul,
so fragrant and perfect were the worshipers,
like a garden club arrangement of rare bulbs.
What I wanted was a field at dusk,
with dandelions leaning in the breeze.

In the evening there were always those
grown wildly alone. When Raymond
turned slowly into the aisle, leaned
doubled on his cane, unable to go on;

when Billy Reed's mother,
a sad, bent woman
who had gone so far into silence, sang,

then the world's true music touched ours,
all the windows of the old church open in June
to the mournful barks, fast whispers of tires.

The Beginning of Heaven

I have dreamed three times of my father
in the year since he died, yet twice he remained
faceless as a shadow:
having struggled from his bed,
he embraced me and vanished through a door;
and he waited like a beggar on the steps—
this was Thanksgiving night—but disappeared
when he tried to give his name.
                              Maybe dreams
were the origin of heaven:
say a man came back as himself,
not an actor in the theater of grief,
but the actual man, with his laughter, his walk;
unmistakably, his hands.
                         Close to dawn,
my father leaned back from the front seat,
holding three wrinkled five-dollar bills,
one for each child, and when his eyes—
absolutely his—grew amused
as we grabbed for the money; when he turned
and cleared his throat once, like a man
prepared to force everyone to listen,
but then simply reached for the key,

I believed we'd continue up the drive,
we'd complete that half-mile ride to the fair,
the giant wheel visible, already, where we were.

Kevin Stein

A Circus of Want

1992

Kevin Stein's most recent collection of poems is *Bruised Paradise* (University of Illinois Press). He has also published a critical study, *James Wright: The Poetry of a Grown Man,* and a book of essays on poetry and history, *Private Poets, Wordly Acts.* He lives in Dunlap, Illinois.

Terms

This night we're drinking beer a pint
at a time, from Ball jars made in Muncie

where my wife and father were born. We're
doing this for no better reason, I think,

than to drink more and drink faster. Nostalgia
plays no part. The evening is coming on.

the low, wide prairie sky has begun to grey
in the fashion that sunsets take in here

when there's 90% humidity and no wind to urge
it elsewhere. No moon yet either, nothing

but the lazy twinkle of a star here and there
and the flashing red elegance of a light

atop the grain elevator. Somewhere beneath it
Varney sits on a three-legged stool with a flashlight

in his hands and a thermos of spiked coffee.
He's waiting for Linda to arrive, no doubt,

so they can move inside where the scales are read,
inside each other's baggy jeans and body, maybe

inside each other's soul. Each Tuesday before Linda
goes out, she wheels her husband to the bedroom,

turns on the television, and kisses him goodbye.
He's memorized this ceremony of the Purple Heart.

knows it as well as any Veterans' Day Parade
he's learned to sit through. Outside his window

and ours, too, a diaphanous fog has risen from the beans,
tempting us to name it good or bad, angel or serpent.

Our black dog pauses in mid-field, surveying
the contour and design of the yellow flashes

that might be earth-bound stars, but are really just
fireflies blinking off and on. The males go high

and the females low while they signal their species
their need, their readiness. All this is true,

but I lied to you earlier. We're drinking
like this because we want a child and we can't

have one. "These things happen," the doctor said,
"These things you have to live with," Most nights

it's easy to feel inadequate, slightly broken,
thinking of the good or even the bad parent

you'll never have the chance to be. Honestly,
we're a little tiresome in our own despair,

which, after all, is not the despair of Varney
when Linda doesn't arrive, or Linda's that she's

not gotten her period, or anything like
that of her husband, who can't lie there

beside her without wanting to touch her
in a way that more than his mind can feel.

The Virgin Birth

Not that I ever believed it, or questioned it,
or really thought about what it

asked me to believe: how someone became
without becoming, how all at once He was,
of a sudden and the flutter of angel's wings,
without the touch of flesh to flesh,
without sweat, without pleasure or the swell
of pleasure that sweat confirms, without
the slightest matting of her unbraided hair
that day when nothing happened to happen
as if something had, as it did for me this morning,
when I whistled through chapped lips
and got nothing—not even the tiniest tune—

but still the dog came at a trot, each footfall
raising a child of dust which disappeared
into our galaxy, an ordinary spiral twirling
about a black hole among another 100 billion
some alien might call *nebulae* if she reads Latin,
or *home* if she's no fool. Why aren't I giddy
with the news every atom of iron in our blood
and calcium in our bones is the gift of a star?
Let me say I'm suspicious, let me say

I have my fears, even though my doubt
is not my father's doubt, bouncing his leg
to Basie's bass line at the Paramount Theatre
in 1939, when the knees of the girl he danced with
held the civilized world in place, sturdy
and predictable as the way she'd surely
clamp them shut. Four years later, hunkered down,
frozen to the frozen tundra of Attu,
he saw those legs kicking wild and open
as Andromeda apologized, invited him in
to the sky of perfect pleasure. It was hard

to believe in anything, let alone
that something could come of nothing,
a god made man to salvage him but not
his Japanese prisoners, their shaved heads

bowed and contemplative, here and there
a wound cherry-red and blooming
with what my father never called "star-stuff,"
though to one he handed his white handkerchief,
and got it back later, decorated,
Mt. Fuji sketched lightly in blood.

Birds in a Circle

I wouldn't argue, either, with the good fortune
of this: a circle of bare dirt, grass and seeds,
the warm jet of air the dryer spills out

to melt the snow. I've seen them perched
in the ash and black locust, among a familiar
stand of blackjack and bur and chinkapin.

Creatures of unreal design—a splotch of blue
or seasonal red, a yellow that's really more green.
They strike the pose of things with wings:

here now, gone now. But seeing them this close,
huddled in a circle of clear space, they look
too-perfectly made, ornaments hand-carved

and painted by my Vietnamese friends—Ly Bao
and Soo Kim, Matthew the son of Lu Ky.
Sometimes the things they make have fooled me:

birds red-bellied and black-capped,
the pileated and ruby-crowned static in mid-flight.
Come here, they say, *Touch me. I won't fly away.*

Still, kneeling in a window above these birds,
I don't move so they won't. This slant of morning,
particular and alluring, tempts me to believe

a thing so lovely it's absurd—that I could live here
forever, if only a wing weren't made for flight,
this body of mine so much dirt.

The WPA in Anderson, Indiana

The elephant had just had enough.
Too many small towns without rivers.
too many tents to raise, the pasha
gone forever. So when he sat down there
on the hood of a Chevy, no one stared.
They had not cared for the ease of his
forgetting a job he was called to do.
Not there in front of Al's Cigars,
the line of unemployed trailing off
to dirty sidewalk.

Now Ginny Marie fusses, and behind us
a row of pocket tee-shirts understands
why she cries. We've filed past
the Peek 'N Booze so many times
no one bothers to look inside. The dancers
make familiar moves, like wives or daughters.
Today is August enough for us, and this one
redbird sings in a tired ailanthus,
its bark split and smelling of stinkwood,
and still he sings.

In Fatima the Virgin appeared, asking
for rosaries. Instead our fathers
worked the WPA, and bent at their waists
they turned the face of this street.
When exhaust rises from cars, we see them
carrying hod. We remember Fifth Street
right side up. the worksong of bricks
turned top for bottom.

It Didn't Begin with Horned Owls Hooting at Noon

Though in them he heard   the weird symmetry
of loss and love's becoming,   a great silence
between one call and the   other's reply.
So he laid block, framed   studs into walls:
plumb, square, on line.   He stayed up late,
straightening bent nails   on the lip of a block
with his ballpeen hammer,   the way a contractor
with a sprung back had shown   him. Evenings
he went next door to talk,   toting his thermos
of bitter coffee and a picture   of his son
who's dying of AIDS. Son   he'd failed, son
he'd pounded on and never got   right. When he
was ready to hang sheet rock,   he penciled on
women with bulbous breasts   and legs
he'd spread wide, women bent   at the waist
as if in supplication to   some irremediable need
only his hand could quiet.   Then he hung
the rock with his women   facing him, sometimes
sawing them in two.   On the morning he finished
he rolled paint over   each and all of them.
Every wall white   in the room where his son,
forgiving him,   was coming home to wait.

A White Lie of Sorrow and Comfort

My daughter's right,
though something's always lost in the telling,
even the glint of surprise
when she told her mother,
"I hugged a bird today."
It goes like this:
the world she hoped for
simply *is*—
the snowfall only a blanket,

those doves merely sleeping
when she presses a frozen bird
against her chest,
that sky a tumble-down grey
and she never guessing.

I've heard what you don't know
can't hurt you.
how a blessed ignorance seals friendships
and preserves marriages,
that happiness can be so beautiful on the branch
you shouldn't pick it,
but I should tell her the one
about her father in a late autumn orchard,
when the last McIntosh hung round and perfect,

so lovely I reached from below
expecting fullness,
but got instead a shell nearly hollow
from the diligence of bees—
an apple as airy as a whiffle ball—
and buzzing, sated bees,
brawling, cider-drunk, cross-eyed,
ready to defend all trespass,
most assuredly mine;
so when I cocked my arm to throw,
one, peering into my ear,
saw an apple canal and launched itself.

O what's the use?
I'm still wondering what's the lesson,
the beauty or the sting of it—
as if anything might come
of anything not promising both.
I'm wondering as if wondering weren't the answer.
the gradual dispatch of the world we trust,
the song of elision even angels can't sing,
a throaty cry, our cry.

Gregory Donovan

Calling His Children Home

1993

Gregory Donovan was born in Mammoth Springs, Arkansas, and raised in Missouri. He teaches at Virginia Commonwealth University, where he helped to establish the graduate creative writing program.

Ragman: 1958
— *"Every goodbye ain't gone."*

That haunt stands up rocking as he boats down
the dream-city in his song, raising sand, raising
Chicago, darktown Memphis, some sweet old
Kokomo, hoofing it down another cobbled alley
in the minded, unswept back channels of his own
St. Louis, and mine, becoming ours again as he

swims back into view among weathered unraveled
       things,
the castoffs he'll tip into a burlap sweat-
stained ragbag. He gathers and knots the sack
shut while the blindered mule nods *yes yes*
at every slipped step, shaking the worn
traces, familiar and forgotten until he jerks
the long reins, taking the last turn,
turning off into music, hollow whomps, jingling.

Bring him back. I can take it now, the stiff
shocks thrown right to the tooth-tip
up from the steel rims grinding, the driven
rhythms beating their wide black wings up
again into the songs he wraps around him,
the private hummings, throat-broken riffs

warmer than the blanket-lined denim jacket
(its corduroy collar is buttoned now at my throat)
torn when he's brought down by the heart's hatcheting.
He makes no sound, no one sees a scarecrow
tip, fall, pitch like a tall pine from the wagon
where he's always stood, bent legs dancing with no
visible effort, timing his song to that beating
he takes every day, swaying in its wooden
scream—in no one's eyes he's driven down, passed
out. The mule slides, stops short, twitching

its long ears, backsteps, jerking, leans down, unhurried
now, lightly troubled, nosing at the man buried
in the shape of his clothes, taking in, switching
easy as any shadow into the angled posture of the lost.

And nobody who has been a pale backyard moon-face
for his passing, becomes somebody, myself, entering
the forbidden alley, walking to the man
lying there knocked out by the sun.
I count my breaths and his to ten,
then put my hand into the man's hand.
He stirs, black wings flapping around us,
wings of the black man's heart rising, catching
again the rhythm of flight, finding his place.

He sits up, stares into my face. The mule
looks away. Wings stir the dust and heat,
snuff whatever words a boy and ragpicker
might have saved from the trash for each other.
He puts his left hand to my shoulder, feels
for the wheel's splintered spokes with his right,

heaves himself up. The man puts my hand inside
his again. Then takes off his coat, wraps
its bruised blues around me. The mule's brown eye,
and the man's, give back no blue-eyed image of me;
black holes that take in every scrap, salt it away.
His eye wants to glance about; he stops himself.
Then he mounts without looking back, whips
up the sleepy mule, and they drag themselves

away toward the last turn again, back to the unseen
work, sailing the same uncharted beat, same old song
and dance, hard at it, counting out the buck and wing
in the measured breaths of a kind of soul that's gone.

Rural Electrification

*"If you put a light on every farm
you put a light in every heart."*
                    —REA official, 1939

In the evening heat they come together,
rugged individualists, the paradoxical
hard-working men and women,
sun scored deep in their skins' folds,
sparked by the chance to claim a share
in whatever power they hold in common,
who as a matter of faith hate all sneaking
communists—and believe by God in the REA.

The bleached revivalist tent has been
raised up again in the fairgrounds dust
to hold the Annual Meeting,
to whip up some kind of spirit
for ceremonies which have lately become
suspicious, which many believe
have lost all meaning. In the hard times,
poor as dirt, they fought spite lines,
high-rates rumors spread by the college boys,
the saboteurs of the big utilities.
Hicks, my grandmother says, is what
they call us now, fooling around
with a hired country band from town,
some half-baked joky magician,
drawings for appliances and junk.
Something's wrong, she says, we're the ones
electrified America. And now we've lost
control, the bosses taking over.
But you watch: no one's out of the tent
when officers are elected.
Young folks don't know. *You'd think
electricity come out of thin air* .

No stockholder, a slick from the city,
and young, I'm standing outside when
the lights come on, part of the show, stealing
shades from the early dark, laying out
shadows hard as a farmer's palm slapped
flat on a table, laying down the law,
setting the limit on what a body can take.

One comes out of that sudden night, gentle
on the arms of friends, the lineman
they have known all his life.

An old boy near me, seeing my face twist
when that man's shape passes into the glare,
and knowing me then for a stranger, begins
without turning, brotherly, shifting the chaw
in his cheek, to tell the story again, how
the lineman climbed up in the tower's hum,
not thinking what he was doing, maybe
reckless just that one time
with the sight of starlings all at once
turning north in the distance, that fine-toothed
edge sawing at the late ice in spring,
and something else in the air, maybe
a buzzard, far up, hung at the tower's peak—
yes maybe he watched those wings, high,
veer, and turning to look for them again
he allowed that line to lightly touch
his naked ear.
        It bit him quick, burning in
that first discovery: *something's wrong,*
he jerked up, rigid, becoming himself
wholly the live wire, the heart-stopping
conductor, giving it everything
as power drove down into his jaw,
chattering wild prophecy, damnation for all,
no way to live with all that shining sap
rising in him needing somewhere to go,

he saw the bolt arc, fire and smoke
shot from his right hand, that riveting
grip lost its hold, let him drop,
the hand gone. The ear burned clean
away. He sagged in the harness, falling
out of his senses, met his death
swimming up at him. Then his dead heart
came back on. Delirious for days,
blinded, no feeling in his body,
he sent away his wife and mother,
would not speak to his children.
He had just two words left: *river, sky.*

Tonight, we can take a burnt man's offering.
We can walk to the pole in the darkest corner
of the night-bounded dooryard, feel for, flick
a switch and a barn will appear out there,
slick as silk from a black tuxedo sleeve.
And we can have this crackling amplified music
so we can stomp our feet against the dark.

Tonight they come for him with the familiar
phrases, *How you doing? Making it all right?*
He smiles, hearing of the chair they've saved,
wants them to know he's better now.
They gently touch him, drawn by the marks
he wears, amazed he's still there
among them to take into the light.

Sarah Henry, Phantom Wife: 1775

It is the cool light in the white room
in the white voice of the lizard.
It is black flies banging at the pane.
It is the grey and silver tensed in the spider's web
and the hoarfrost sparkling in the brittle grasses.
It is the shuttered moon in the reptile eye.

It is a woman buried to her breasts
in the damp of the earth rolling away
from her place in a window in the ground
where she waits in the hard white dress
for the cloak, the dark buttoned trousers to mount
three stone steps into nothing with its red carriage
      wheels.

It is the rustling in the petticoats of a daughter,
it is the silence in the skirts of a slave.
It is a woman spreading her hair to dry
over the bent-backed chair before the fire.
The woman believes at times she can see its shadow
thrown against the wall, whirling and beating,
the squealing engine of the madness of the times.
The lizard says no mirrors here.
Mistress Henry has developed *a strange antipathy*.
It is a woman jumping up like a spark fading out.

In the wood above her head, demons busy
with their work, knocking and laughing,
sometimes dancing to the lizard's fiddle tunes
and eating the good food she gets cold.
Mistress of demons, fed on air and candles.
Soon, soon, they moan, and promise to leave her
to slip into the unmarked grave of her long dream.
It is waking in the scratch of her name across a deed.
It is the leg crushed in the accident at the mill.
After it was cut off, the hired man said he felt it
again at night, a phantom lying beside him in bed.

What makes a man think he can own anything?

The lizard steps from his trapdoor in the smoke,
scales of smoke-grey tipped with smoke-black, candle
in hand, leaving the pewter tankard to warm
on the andiron shelf, checking her bonds, taking off
his powdered hair, his one blue horn jutting . . .
If broken off, she has been told, it simply grows back.

The lizard eyes dart their many directions.
The swift lizard says sometimes the wrong herb
will make its way into the soup's shining face,
sometimes the lovely arched fireplace will smoke.
The lizard says he will set her free. A lizard's head
bobs up and down. Shoulders, too. Up and down.

It is a husband at night burying a wife in shame
like a dog in the open field, snakebit
yet given, he may assure himself, *every loving care.*
The master, Patrick, swears never to speak her name
        again.
It is a man burning wax myrtle candles, the strait-dress
smoldering on the fire in an empty basement room.
Sarah, name of his mother, name of the dead.
It is a name whispered, broken off. It grows back.

Nietzsche in the Engadine

White fog, white flakes come rolling and roar
through the surging black pines. Somewhere
in that storm wild horses wheel and plunge.
And somewhere shines my bright and lucky star.
No. Revise. I will not have it icy cold.
This I, who has never in his life been able to afford
enough coal. So it will be summer, cool,
we will allow the pines their green. I am
walking with my sister arm in arm. No. Not that
treachery. I will be a silkworm hung in the mulberry tree.

The winter storm comes again. To blast
against the burn of my aching head.
Do not look into the snowstorm's heart—
all the many souls on the wind, each
with its little burden bringing it to ground,
to the trample of wheels and shod hooves.
Do not look, your soul flies out, dances away

on the patterned gusts, leaving you an empty
page to lie down, buried in the book of snow.
And I write such books, don't I?

At the edge of the river rubbing its hands
over its foaming stones, stands a tree
bursting in gold leaf. It is the perfect
image of my brain. Snow spills past,
blurring the outline of its brooding fan.
Trees on the far bank disappear in the building
storm. Strange my brain has moved there, leaving me
strange peace as it goes on seeding the wind . . .

The fox carries himself like a secret knowledge.
A shadow blooms in the red idea trailing him,
the gaudy cloud that dogs his every step,
that tail of winter air, not fur!

Four days I have not been able to compose my face.
I go about the village grinning, my inspired clowning.

But in the brothel of Cologne, I touched nothing
but the piano. Those creatures of tinsel and gauze
fled at the sound of my first chords.

This morning, a cab driver was beating the eyes
of his horse in the piazza. I threw my arms
over the animal's neck. The driver kept up
his cursing and whipping until I collapsed
in the street, a delicious melody rising lightly
from the space between the cobblestones, a music
from the hidden world, suitable for strings.
Waking, I rushed to the piano, discovered
it was stinging in my fingertips, I
raced toward it, faster and playing faster
that wild song until they took it away.

In two months I shall be the foremost name
on earth. But for now I am a rider of trains.

Over the white meadow the railway drives
deeper and higher into the forest, leaving
the broken star cast over the snowfield,
running faster, leaving mother, lover, autumn,
driving on into the storm's heart,
to the cemetery on the hill, the grave by the wall
where the father waits with the brother in his arms.

I am safe only in mountains.
I am every name in history, covered in snow.
And the one name, the small blue stone
nestled in its wooden box, sealed with the kiss
of animal lips on his outstretched palm
like a handful of matches in flames.

George Bilgere

The Going

1994

George Bilgere teaches at John Carroll University in Cleveland, Ohio. He is currently at work on a book of poems about his experiences as a Fulbright Fellow in Spain in 1992.

Healing

The girl I love still sleeps with her mother
who is huge, bulky as a bear.
It is a small house in Guthrie
without a doorknob or a father,
He is silent on a hill. They forget
to leave flowers on Memorial Day.

We stay up late, kissing in the car,
windows open to the cricket buzz.
Inside, her mother barely sleeps.
Food goes bad in the fridge.
The worthless brother, guitar
plugged to the wall, wails.

The boom's gone bust.
Every other house
is empty in this neighborhood,
a democracy of failure.
Armadillos rustle in the brush.
We watch the neighbors tune their truck,
the legs of a woman they saw
in a bar last night troubling
the pure mechanics of their talk.

All day the brother sleeps
in his leaking waterbed.
Bombers smolder from the base.
The father, a stern man
in uniform, watches me
from the bookshelf.

Her hair sweet
with the smell of permanent,
is black as oil, and the lines
her nails leave down my spine

are red as Oklahoma roads.
In the sink her dishes grow
green. The backyard rises
in a weedy funk, foaming
over bones of old cars.
The dog drowns in ticks.

An aunt comes by, ashen-faced.
This is a laying on of hands.
Her tumor's growing like a great idea,
a central concept. *Jesus*
everyone says, their palms
burning through to the core. *Heal*
A cousin wears Christ
on a T-shirt: *This blood's for you.*
Pepsi's in the fridge.

Soaps in the afternoon, couples
humping through the broadcast day
In the glamor magazines
scattered on the floor
women tan and tone.
They come hard with famous men.
I suggest we go

for a doorknob at the hardware store.
Vetoed. Too hot.
A sister visits, baby
sucking at her chest.
She swears her milk
will shoot across the room.

At dusk we go to the Sonic,
a neon bonfire near
the base's barbed perimeter.
B-52s tilt over with a black wake.
Evil, she says, munching okra
her face so beautiful
in the red fire of sunset

my throat tightens, I could cry.
A song comes over the radio,
the very car shimmers, the bulbs
of the drive-in blooming
red and blue, deepening
in the failing light
and she moves into my arms.
smelling of soap and french fries.
All around us
men and women, boys and girls,
are tuned to the same frequency,
moving together under the tinted glass,
beneath the whirlwind of moths
in the hot air, the Sonic
throbbing with light and love,
the life I left to come here
forgotten and the sun
sliding down a dome of gold.
She laughs. Mosquitoes
rise in the rural haze.
Her tongue is in my ear.

6 O'Clock

I remember the late rain
Darkened the hills close by
But far from where they let me play.
There came always, on those afternoons,
Forlorn cannonades of thunder,
Lightning too wan to brighten
The tense corridors of our house.

When the light was low she would say
He's coming home , and I
Would think of him in his white shirt
And dark tie, amber glass in hand,
The bruise of whiskey on the air.

And the day I remember was like
All the days, when the round black car,
Rain streaming from its flanks,
Rolled back home from his office somewhere,
Gliding through the storm, down
My father's angry will, to stop
Before the house like nightfall.

We heard the door slam. I saw his shoulders
Bunch against the fusillade of rain.
Daddy' s home , she cried in her tight voice
And ran from me to the hallway
To struggle a moment in his arms.
He let her down, then came for me.

Exiles

The management was hell on birds.
August brought a rain of dead pigeons
winding up their flight on the asphalt
five floors down while my father sat
shirtless in the air-conditioned room,
the TV's bad nerve throbbing all day.
We watched westerns, hiding out like bandits.
The scotch bottle glowed like a yellow bulb.
Nice bird, he said, touching the dry,
iridescent mantle of a corpse I carried in.
Now get the damn thing out of here.
Then he made a few calls—he was a powerful man—
and the pigeons stopped falling. That's what
I remember, how my father could speak a word
into the phone, even then, when everyone
had stopped listening. and suddenly
the sky would be full of birds again.

Wanton Boys

He raised an air gun to the trees
and let it spit, so all of us could squat
in the dust around the stiffened sparrow
to fathom meanings in its swift descent.
In a closed garage one afternoon
we used a drill press to punch hole
after slippery hole in a box turtle's
tight-lipped shell, its agony received
privately and without complaint.
Cats doused with gasoline and set ablaze
shot like comets over the dark fields.
The pigeon blinded and thrown to the sky
climbed enormous stairs of terror
like a dare, like mud in God's eye.
The gut-shot rabbits limping off to hide
and dogs whipped hard for the simple joy
of hearing their cries turn human
informed all beasts of our dominion.
Even the Great Horned Owl, after a pair
of bolt cutters trimmed its wings to stumps,
hopped about like a silly harmless frog.
Meanwhile the girls stayed home and dressed
their dolls. Good Lord, they began to bleed
before we ever laid a hand on them.

Zones of Embarkation

The first sign is the smell of fresh paint in the hallways
opening onto the courtyard where the Virgin stands
in her cloak of moss, and the fronds of thin palms
gleam in their green enamel. There is a rush of color,
a time of bright change and transition.
The buzz of saws arises from the basements, and the
     years

trapped in the wood's rigor release a cheerful tang.
Then comes the clangor of hammers, of light beating the
        hillsides
into spring with a steady, fascinated concentration.
You have the pleasant sense that things love themselves.
Even the ground is humming with it, and the sailors
on the river, bareheaded in their sun-bleached ship,
are hot with destinations. At this point the villagers
discern a slight shudder. Far off, a church strikes noon
and everything starts unmooring in a din of panic.
It is in some respects a kind of mass deportation,
a rough strife of engines and lamentation,
although no one realizes it at the time.
Nonetheless: details first, then cities and even whole
        years
are hauled off in the dust and silvery light.
Television screens go black as old roses
and great chunks and grids blank out without ceremony,
the kind of thing that always goes wrong with
        computers,
although it isn't a mistake, exactly. Someone I love
waits barefoot by the sea, alarmed by distant flames,
her blue-veined ankles bathed in foam. Sheep on green
        hills
beyond the office window flee into their own
        imaginations.
The beauty of the least gesture is at last apparent.
Somehow, thoughts of far-off landfalls give small
        consolation.
I see her bend, glinting in gold, to tie her sandals.
In my haste I always forget to wave.

The Going

Our mother had no use for God
but loved to fry a mountain
of onion rings on Sunday night

and play Scrabble with us
while the TV shed
its gray light from the corner.
Mystery was what
the hard wooden chips,
face down in their cardboard box,
would turn up as we built
our intersections of words,
brief structures that the flipped
board destroyed at midnight.

I can see her, beyond
the surf's roar, going from pool
to pool at low tide, prodding
anemones to make their mouths
tighten like wombs, stroking
the suede-backed starfish,
looking up sometimes to stare
emptily out to sea.
She was young enough to run
when the waves broke
like milk against the coral;
and now, in the gray dawn,
I can almost hear her
warning us of the suck and tumble
until my own voice answers
and drowns beneath the breakers.

She would have laughed to see us
so ceremonious and solemn,
reaching into the box
to cast the ashes to the foam,
sowing the deafening Pacific
with her flame-tempered particles,
as if we could give our mother back.

Collections of Poetry Published by the University of Missouri Press 1960-1996

* Denotes Devins Award winner

1960 Thomas McAfee, *Poems and Stories*

1965 Nancy Sullivan, *The History of the World as Pictures**

1966 Saul Touster, *Still Lives and Other Lives**

1967 Nancy Willard, *Skin of Grace**
Thomas McAfee, *I'll Be Home Late Tonight*
George Garrett, *For a Bitter Season: New and Selected Poems*

1968 Edsel Ford, *Looking for Shiloh**
Lewis Turco, *Awaken, Bells Falling: Poems 1959–1967*

1969 John Calvin Rezmerski, *Held for Questioning**

1970 John Bennett, *The Struck Leviathan: Poems on "Moby Dick"**
R. P. Dickey, *Acting Immortal*

1971 Henry Carlile, *The Rough-Hewn Table**
Dorothy Hughes, *The Great Victory Mosaic*

1972 Jonathan Holden, *Design for a House**

1973 Ed Ochester, *Dancing on the Edges of Knives**
Darcy Gottlieb, *No Witness But Ourselves*

1974 Gerald Costanzo, *In the Aviary**
Annie Dillard, *Tickets for a Prayer Wheel*

1975   Daniel J. Langton, *Querencia**
      James J. McAuley, *After the Blizzard*
      Roger K. Meiners, *Journeying Back to the World*
      Peter Cooley, *The Company of Strangers*

1976   Diana O'Hehir, *Summoned**
      Joseph di Prisco, *Wit's End*
      Willis Barnstone, *China Poems*

1977   C. G. Hanzlicek, *Stars**
      Jonathan Aldrich, *Croquet Lover at the Dinner Table*

1978   Janet Beeler, *Dowry**

1979   G. E. Murray, *Repairs**

1980   Frank Manley, *Resultances**

1981   no Devins Award given
      Ronald Wallace, *Plums, Stones, Kisses & Hooks*

1982   Mary Kinzie, *The Threshold of the Year**

1983   Harry Humes, *Winter Weeds**
      Kathryn Hankla, *Phenomena*

1984   Wesley McNair, *The Faces of Americans in 1853**
      Robert Gibb, *The Winter House*
      Richard Robbins, *The Invisible Wedding*

1985   Jane O. Wayne, *Looking Both Ways**

1986   Shirley Bowers Anders, *The Bus Home**

1987   Nancy Schoenberger, *Girl on a White Porch**

1988   Penelope Wilkinson Austin, *Waiting for a Hero**

1989   Richard Lyons, *These Modern Nights**

1990   John Repp, *Thirst Like This**

1991   Judson Mitcham, *Somewhere in Ecclesiastes**
Stephanie Strickland, *Give the Body Back*
Heather R. Miller, *Hard Evidence*
Judy Ruiz, *Talking Razzmatazz*

1992   Kevin Stein, *Circus of Want**
Miller Williams, *Adjusting to the Light*
Stephen Corey, *All These Lands You Call One Country*
Michael Blumenthal, *The Wages of Goodness*

1993   Gregory Donovan, *Calling His Children Home**
Heather Ross Miller, *Friends and Assassins*
Robert Gibb, *Fugue for a Late Snow*
Howard Nemerov, *A Howard Nemerov Reader*
James Whitehead, *Near at Hand*

1994   George Bilgere, *The Going**
C. G. Hanzlicek, *Against Dreaming*
Patricia Traxler, *Forbidden Words*
Michael Burns, *Secret Names*

1995   Maurya Simon, *Golden Labyrinth*
David Swanger, *This Waking Unafraid*

1996   Dabney Stuart, *Poems for Paintings by Carroll Cloar*

Judges Who Selected
the Devins Award Winners
(alphabetical order)

Robert Boyers
Bruce Cutler
Deborah Digges
Paul Engle
Irving Feldman
Edward Field
Donald Finkel
George Garrett
Margaret Gibson
Michael S. Harper
Donald Justice
X. J. Kennedy
Carolyn Kizer
John Knoepfle
Thomas McAfee
William Peden
Winfield Townley Scott
William Stafford
Mark Strand
Dabney Stuart
Hollis Summers
May Swenson
Henry Taylor
David Wagoner
Harold Whitehall
Reed Whittemore
Richard Wilbur

Permissions

Poems from Devins Award-winning titles are reprinted here with the courtesy of their authors as follows:

From *The History of the World as Pictures:* "The History of the World as Pictures," "Prehistoric Cave Painting of a Bison," "Las Meninas by Velazquez (1656)," "Number 1 by Jackson Pollock (1948)," "Money," "In the Fields," "The House by the Sea," "What Time?," and "He Has No Personal Life" are reprinted by permission of Nancy Sullivan.

From *Still Lives and Other Lives*: "Green Apple: Still Life I," "Green Apple: Still Life II," "Green Apple: Still Life iii," "Kafka's Funeral," "Lunch Hour Idyll," "Vision," and three sections from "Salo, The Artist" are reprinted by permission of Saul Touster.

From *Held for Questioning*: "Supplement to an Ethic," "Animism II," "American Motives," "Courtship and Conquest," "A Posteriori," "Pragmatism," "Guest of Honor," "Fossil," and "Fall Morning" are reprinted by permission of John Calvin Rezmerski.

From *The Struck Leviathan: Poems on "Moby Dick"*: "*Ishmael:* Loomings, Christmas Day, Late," "*Father Mapple:* On the Abyss of the Godhead," "*Ishmael:* In the Crow's Nest," "*Ahab:* At His Cabin Window, Midnight," "*Bulkington:* The Struck Leviathan," "*Ishmael:* The Pod," "*Ahab:* Near the Mainmast, Sunrise," "*Ishmael:* Death of Ahab," and "*Ishmael:* 'Pequod' Down" are reprinted by permission of the Estate of John Bennett.

From *The Rough-Hewn Table*: "Grandmother," "Three for the Predators," "The Job," "Three Monu-